The Lunar Nodes

Unlock the Secrets of the Navagrahas, Your Birth Chart, Karma, the Sun and Moon in Astrology, and the Twelve Houses of the Zodiac

© Copyright 2024 - All rights reserved.

The content contained within this book may not be reproduced, duplicated, or transmitted without direct written permission from the author or the publisher.

Under no circumstances will any blame or legal responsibility be held against the publisher, or author, for any damages, reparation, or monetary loss due to the information contained within this book, either directly or indirectly.

Legal Notice:

This book is copyright protected. It is only for personal use. You cannot amend, distribute, sell, use, quote, or paraphrase any part, or the content within this book, without the consent of the author or publisher.

Disclaimer Notice:

Please note the information contained within this document is for educational and entertainment purposes only. All effort has been executed to present accurate, up-to-date, reliable, and complete information. No warranties of any kind are declared or implied. Readers acknowledge that the author is not engaging in the rendering of legal, financial, medical, or professional advice. The content within this book has been derived from various sources. Please consult a licensed professional before attempting any techniques outlined in this book.

By reading this document, the reader agrees that under no circumstances is the author responsible for any losses, direct or indirect, that are incurred as a result of the use of the information contained within this document, including, but not limited to, errors, omissions, or inaccuracies.

Your Free Gift
(only available for a limited time)

Thanks for getting this book! If you want to learn more about various spirituality topics, then join Mari Silva's community and get a free guided meditation MP3 for awakening your third eye. This guided meditation mp3 is designed to open and strengthen ones third eye so you can experience a higher state of consciousness. Simply visit the link below the image to get started.

https://spiritualityspot.com/meditation

Or, Scan the QR code!

Table of Contents

INTRODUCTION 1
CHAPTER 1: THE BASICS OF VEDIC ASTROLOGY 2
CHAPTER 2: WHAT ARE THE NAVAGRAHAS? 21
CHAPTER 3: WHAT ARE THE LUNAR NODES? 35
CHAPTER 4: RAHU AND KETU IN THE ZODIAC SIGNS 55
CHAPTER 5: RAHU AND KETU IN THE TWELVE HOUSES 64
CHAPTER 6: KARMIC LESSONS 81
CHAPTER 7: BIRTH CHART SAMPLES 92
CHAPTER 8: DECODING YOUR BIRTH CHART 100
CHAPTER 9: ASTROLOGICAL REMEDIES 123
BONUS CHAPTER: GLOSSARY OF TERMS 136
CONCLUSION 148
HERE'S ANOTHER BOOK BY MARI SILVA THAT YOU MIGHT LIKE 149
YOUR FREE GIFT (ONLY AVAILABLE FOR A LIMITED TIME) 150
REFERENCES 151

Introduction

If you love to delve into astrology, you probably already know everything you need to know about your birth chart. You'll know about your Moon, Sun, and Rising sign, and you likely read your horoscope daily. How else will you know what the day will bring?

Even so, no matter how much cosmic knowledge you have, you probably know that something is still missing from your life or something isn't resonating. You may have been born during the season of Taurus but feel more like an Aries. Were you born on the cusp? That could be one reason, but there is another; you probably use Western astrology when you should be using Vedic astrology.

This guide will teach you all you need to know about Vedic astrology and how the Lunar Nodes feature in your life. You'll understand Rahu and Ketu, how they fit into the 12 houses and the Zodiac signs, and you'll also learn how to read your birth chart according to Vedic astrology.

I promise that "The Lunar Nodes" will teach you far more than any other book on the same subject. Why? Because it's written in plain, simple English, with full explanations of everything and step-by-step guides where needed.

Read on if you want to learn more about Vedic astrology and how the lunar nodes affect you and your life. This is one journey you will truly enjoy.

Chapter 1: The Basics of Vedic Astrology

Modern astrology comes from an Ancient Greek word, "astrología," which means the study of the stars. More specifically, it means studying planet and star movement to see their influence over events on Earth, including how they affect individual people. Astrology in all its many forms has been studied and practiced since the beginning of human civilization, and this chapter will explore one of those forms – Vedic astrology.

Vedic Astrology Origins

Humans have been studying Vedic astrology since before history was first recorded. For example, a calendrical system reliant on the accurate moon, planet, and star tracking was used by ancient Indians, and the Mahabharata, an ancient Indian epic more than 5000 years old, includes plenty of references to astrology, including calculations and signs. However, astrology wasn't just used to determine destiny and character and for planting and harvesting, planning festivals, weddings, and more.

An astrology system virtually the same as the ancient Indian system was used worldwide. The Babylonian Empire of the 3rd and 2nd Millenia BC in the Middle East helped predict major events and natural disasters, while the Mayan Empire, 2nd Millennium BC, designed their temples on planetary movements.

Mayans designed their temples based on planetary movements.
Ricraider, CC BY-SA 3.0 <https://creativecommons.org/licenses/by-sa/3.0>, via Wikimedia Commons: https://commons.wikimedia.org/wiki/File:Mayan_Temple_of_the_Sun.jpg

However, one event involving astrology stands head and shoulders above all else – the birth of Jesus Christ. Three astrologers looking to the heavens saw a celestial sign indicating the birth of a king of kings. By studying the skies and accurately interpreting the planetary and stellar positions, they determined when and where he would be born.

Today, astrology is used by many different cultures to determine festival and holiday dates and the passage of time. Many traditions, including Islam, Judaism, and Hinduism, use a lunar calendar to determine their holy days.

How Vedic Astrology Works

It's fair to say that astrology is one of the most sophisticated and complex sciences. Astrologers use centuries of applied and theoretical knowledge to interpret how the stars and planets are arranged to determine specific events on Earth. The rest of this chapter will provide an overview of key astrological elements: zodiac signs, twelve houses, and the planets. This is just a basic look; you'll learn more about these throughout the rest of the book.

The 12 Zodiac Signs

Despite being a three-dimensional space, all planets in the solar system orbit along one single plane – the ecliptic. Throughout this orbit, every planet will also pass through the constellations. Astrology explains twelve signs or constellations divide the 360-degree orbit into 12 sections, each 30 degrees. These sections are the zodiac signs.

Each sign has its own symbol and personality determined by a set of specific characteristics. Each could be considered a specific type of environment the planets go through in their orbit. You should also know that the signs are all ruled by a specific planet, so each planet is "home" when it passes through its own sign.

Let's look at each sign, their rulers, symbols, and domains:

SIGN	PLANETARY RULER	SYMBOL	CHIEF DOMAINS
Aries	Mars	♈ - the Ram	Leadership Playfulness A sense of purpose Self-confidence Competition

SIGN	PLANETARY RULER	SYMBOL	CHIEF DOMAINS
Taurus	Venus	♉ - the Bull	Loyalty Thoughtfulness Determination The arts Sensuality
Gemini	Mercury	♊ - the Twins	Charm Communication Imagination Logic Curiosity
Cancer	The Moon	♋ - the Crab	Compassion Creativity Sensitivity Emotions Motherhood
Leo	The Sun	♌ - the Lion	Dignity Ambition Power Nobility Authority
Virgo	Mercury	♍ - the Virgin	Intelligence Resourcefulness Modesty Courtesy Service

SIGN	PLANETARY RULER	SYMBOL	CHIEF DOMAINS
Libra	Venus	♎ - the Scales	Justice Balance Aesthetics Ethics Optimism
Scorpio	Mars	♏ - the Scorpion	Criticism Secrets Harshness Mystery Intensity
Sagittarius	Jupiter	♐ - the Archer	Wisdom Good fortune Spirituality Religion Virtue
Capricorn	Saturn	♑ - the Goat	Philosophy Deliberation Stubbornness Discipline Skepticism
Aquarius	Saturn	♒ - the Water Bearer	Social justice Altruism Idealism Patience Renunciation

SIGN	PLANETARY RULER	SYMBOL	CHIEF DOMAINS
Pisces	Jupiter	♓ - the Fishes	Depth Shyness Knowledge Mysticism Beauty

The Twelve Houses

So, you now know that the planetary orbit is divided into 12 sections, each a specific zodiac sign. The sky is also divided into 12 - 6 in the sky you can see and 6 in the sky you cannot see because it's on the other side of the Earth.

Unlike the signs moving through the night sky, the 12 houses are fixed. In simple terms, the first house will always start on the Eastern Horizon and the seventh on the Western horizon - that never changes. Each house also rules over a certain part of human life:

House	Position	Body Part	Domains
First	Eastern horizon to 30 degrees below	Head	Physical appearance Personality Character Longevity Happiness
Second	30 to 60 degrees below the Eastern horizon	Face	Traditions Wealth Education Speech Generosity

House	Position	Body Part	Domains
Third	60 to 90 degrees below the Eastern horizon	Neck Shoulders Hands Arms	Courage Siblings Literature Virtue Sports
Fourth	60 to 90 degrees below the Western horizon	Chest Lungs Heart	Beliefs Vehicles Home Homeland The mother
Fifth	30 to 60 degrees below the Western horizon	Stomach	Creativity Wisdom Children Success Investments
Sixth	Western horizon to 30 degrees below	Intestines Lower abdomen	Fear Disease Debt Service Enemies
Seventh	Western horizon to 30 degrees above	Internal sex organs Colon	Marital happiness Spouse Sexual desire Contracts Faithfulness

House	Position	Body Part	Domains
Eighth	30 to 60 degrees above the Western horizon	Anus Genitals	Scandals Revolutions Calamities Occult Time/cause of death
Ninth	60 to 90 degrees above the Western horizon	Thighs Hips	Religion Piety Morality Spiritual master Destiny
Tenth	60 to 90 degrees above the Eastern horizon	Knees Backs	Career Rank The father Authority Reputation
Eleventh	30 to 60 degrees above the Eastern horizon	Calves	Income Gains Aspirations Marketplaces Communities
Twelfth	Eastern horizon to 30 degrees above	Feet	Misfortune Losses Forgiveness The subconscious Liberation

The Planets

The word planet originated from a Greek word, "planets," which means the wanderer, which is unsurprising since the planets travel at a fixed pace along a defined orbit in space. Astrology explains that every planet has its own personality and characteristics. Here's an overview of each planet and its primary features:

Planet	Weekday	Travel Speed Through the Zodiac	Portfolio
The Sun	Sunday	One zodiac sign a month	Governments The soul The father Prestige Health
The Moon	Monday	One sign every 2 ½ days	Emotions Creativity Happiness The mother Agriculture The mind
Mars	Tuesday	One sign every 2 months	Warfare Vitality Anger Courage Opposition Enemies

Planet	Weekday	Travel Speed Through the Zodiac	Portfolio
Mercury	Wednesday	One sign a week	Communication Intellect Theater Logic Learning Literature
Jupiter	Thursday	One sign a year	Devotion Wisdom Sons The husband Piety Holy places
Venus	Friday	One sign every 2 ½ weeks	Marriage Sensuality The wife Luxury Aesthetics Music
Saturn	Saturday	One sign every 2 ½ years	Philosophy Obstacles Impiety Poverty Longevity Livelihood

Planet	Weekday	Travel Speed Through the Zodiac	Portfolio
Rahu	None	One sign every 1 ½ years	Swelling Snakes Wickedness Outcastes False arguments Traveling
Ketu	None	One sign every 1 ½ years	Wounds Surrender Salvation Apathy Out-of-body experiences Fever

The 27 Nakshatras

According to Vedic astrology, there are 27 nakshatras, small constellations of stars. The moon travels through these constellations as it makes its orbit around the Earth. The English term for the nakshatras is "the lunar mansions," Vedic astrologers study the nakshatras and zodiac signs together to work out extra details about our inborn traits are also considered essential in Muhurtha (electional astrology) to help determine the right times for significant life events.

Nakshatra	Planetary Ruler	Zodiac Sign	Symbol
Ashwini	Ketu	Aries	Horse's head
Bharani	Venus	Aries	Female sex organ

Nakshatra	Planetary Ruler	Zodiac Sign	Symbol
Krittika	Sun	Aries – 1st quarter Taurus – 2nd, 3rd, and 4th quarters	Flame or knife
Rohini	Moon	Taurus	Temple or oxcart
Mrighashira	Mars	Gemini	Teardrop or human head
Ardra	Rahu	Aries	Horse's head
Punarvasu	Jupiter	Gemini – 1st, 2nd, 3rd quarters Cancer – 4th quarter	Bow and quiver
Pushya	Saturn	Cancer	Circle, lotus, or cow's udder
Ashlesha	Mercury	Cancer	Serpent
Magha	Ketu	Leo	A throne or palanquin
Purva-phalguni	Venus	Leo	Hammock
Uttara-phalguni	Sun	Leo – 1st quarter Virgo – 2nd, 3rd, 4th quarters	Bed

Nakshatra	Planetary Ruler	Zodiac Sign	Symbol
Hasta	Moon	Virgo	Hand
Chitra	Mars	Virgo – $1^{st}, 2^{nd}$ quarter Libra – $3^{rd}, 4^{th}$ quarter	Jewel or pearl
Swati	Rahu	Libra	A blade of fresh grass
Vishakha	Jupiter	Libra – $1^{st}, 2^{nd}, 3^{rd}$ quarters Scorpio – 4th quarter	Potter's wheel
Anuradha	Saturn	Scorpio	Lotus flower
Jyeshta	Mercury	Scorpio	Umbrella
Mula	Ketu	Sagittarius	Roots
Purva-ashadha	Venus	Sagittarius	Winnowing basket
Uttara-ashadha	Sun	Sagittarius – 1st quarter Capricorn – $2^{nd}, 3^{rd}, 4^{th}$ quarters	An elephant's tusk
Shravana	Moon	Capricorn	An ear

Nakshatra	Planetary Ruler	Zodiac Sign	Symbol
Dhanishta	Mars	Capricorn - 1st, 2nd quarters Aquarius - 3rd, 4th quarter	A drum
Shatabhisha	Rahu	Aquarius	Empty circle
Purva-Bhadrapada	Jupiter	Aquarius - 1st, 2nd, 3rd quarters Pisces - 4th quarter	Funeral bed
Uttara-Bhadrapada	Saturn	Pisces	A snake
Revati	Mercury	Pisces	A fish

Different Types of Vedic Astrology

Astrology is used for a lot of different things. Western people are familiar with horoscopes or birth chart readings, but other reading types are used to provide specific information under certain circumstances. These are the most common types of Vedic astrology:

Horoscope Readings

Otherwise known as birth charts, horoscopes are 2D maps of the stellar and planetary positions relative to Earth at a person's time of birth. Taken into consideration are the longitude and latitude of the birth location and the exact time of birth. Horoscopes are powerful tools; when read properly, they accurately foretell significant life events, personality, time of death, past lives, and much more for an individual.

Relationship Compatibility

Relationship readings examine the horoscopes of two people to determine compatibility. This tends to be used more during couple counseling or marriage planning. However, it can also be used for any relationship type - parent/child, friends, teacher/student, boss/employee, etc. These readings are essential to help identify strengths and/or weaknesses in a specific relationship, providing good insight for couples struggling to understand their partner's point of view.

Muhurtha (Electional)

Electional readings, while not used in the West, determine the best time for a major event. Muhurtha readings are useful in the following situations:

- Life events - important ceremonies, falling pregnant, weddings, etc.
- Big purchases - new home, new car, etc.
- Launching new financial ventures or a business
- Long distance travel

Prashna (Horary)

In Prashna astrology, a chart is cast at the exact moment an individual asks a question. This chart is interpreted to provide a conclusive, clear answer to that specific question, which can be about virtually anything. However, the first step is to verify the inquirer's sincerity, signified by the rising sign's qualities and strengths. Horary astrology is commonly used in the following ways:

- To find a lost object or person.
- To inform about a major decision in life.
- To work out when a person will meet the person they will marry.
- To understand what causes an illness and how it can be cured.

Ayurvedic Jyotish (Medical Astrology)

This typically focuses on wellbeing and health and correlates planetary positions and specific astrological factors with health conditions. It also provides insight into remedies, preventative measures, and potential health concerns concerning an individual's birth chart. It is typically used with Ayurvedic medicine as a complementary approach.

Vastu Shastra

Vastu Shastra is a science born in ancient India and is related to architecture, dimensions, and space; the aim is to ensure living areas are fully aligned with the cosmic energies, balancing them and bringing harmony. Vedic astrology plays a role in Vastu Shastra; it helps determine the placement, direction, and arrangement of a building's elements. It can also be used on plots of land.

Janma Kundli (Natal Astrology)

The most common Vedic astrology form, Janma Kundli, revolves around creating a birth chart for an individual, providing insight into their strengths, weaknesses, characteristics, life events, and personality.

Karma

You've all heard of Karma – it's a case of what goes around, comes around. In other words, everything you do will come back to you in this life or the next one. According to Hinduism, three types of Karma exist:

- **Prarabdha** – all the Karma accumulated in your current lifetime.
- **Sanchita** – the sum of all Karma from your past lives.
- **Agami** – this results from current decisions and actions.

However, most people talk about good and bad Karma. You get good Karma when you do positive things in your life, i.e., helping those in need, while bad Karma comes when you do negative things, such as stealing from someone, hurting others, etc.

The 12 Laws of Karma

Are you starting to see a pattern yet? 12 zodiac signs, 12 houses, and now the 12 laws of Karma. Think of these laws as the rules of the Karma game. They help you understand how it works. According to the Buddhist and Hindu belief systems, the laws help you interpret how energy works within the universe, and they help you to understand how actions affect others, yourself, and the universe.

1. **The Great Law:** the most commonly known; this law states that you get back what you put out. You will receive kindness and love if you put out kindness and love.
2. **The Law of Creation:** don't wait for things to happen to you. Get out there and make it happen.
3. **The Law of Humility:** changing anything in your current life means accepting the current state of things. That means accepting who you are before you can change anything in this life or the next.
4. **The Law of Growth:** this law is about internal growth, change, and evolution. As you change internally, you change externally too. This means taking the time to learn new things, heal, and change.

5. **The Law of Responsibility:** as you would expect, this law revolves around owning what happens in your life - good and bad. Only you can choose your life, and you are responsible for what you do and say, how you act, and how you treat others.
6. **The Law of Connection:** people are connected to each other and everything. While your past- present- and future-you may appear different, they are all still the same person. Whatever you do will lead to something different. Thus, it is all interlinked, and you are linked to other people, too.
7. **The Law of Focus:** This law tells you you can't think of more than one thing at a time. When you focus on one thing only, like spiritual values, you can't focus on anything negative simultaneously.
8. **The Law of Giving and Hospitality:** this tells you to stop preaching and start doing. At some time in your life, you will be asked to prove that you do what you say. Let's say you are thinking of decluttering your home and donating some of your belongings to a charitable cause; instead of thinking about it, get on and do it. If you can't walk the walk, don't talk the talk.
9. **The Law of Here and Now** is about getting out of the past and into the present. Stop dwelling on what was and live what is now.
10. **The Law of Change:** some people feel like they experience something bad repeatedly, but they could be attracting bad luck. It's a sign. The Universe tells you to make changes in your life. Until you do, the pattern repeats until you finally sit up and take note.
11. **The Law of Patience and Reward** tells you that your hard work will eventually pay off. Provided you show up and pitch in and don't give up on your goals, even when it seems like all is lost, the rewards will come. Patience pays dividends, so live your life and celebrate every achievement, be it small or large.
12. **The Law of Significance and Inspiration:** the last law tells you that everyone is significant. Everyone has some value to share with others and can positively impact the world.

Past Life Karma Vedic Astrology

Vedic astrology is important in how each individual is, as it records all their past Karma. The association with Karma is that Vedic astrology predicts emotion and physical growth, and anything that a person may experience due to past life Karma. Many people believe that a person cannot fully control their current life because of astrology and Karma.

Vedic astrology helps us identify three different types of Karma – fixed, not-so-fixed medium, and the one being made right now with everything you think and do. Vedic astrology also shows the planetary positions at the exact time of an individual's birth. It explains the planetary periods, or Dasha, used to interpret good and bad life phases.

Later chapters will discuss dashas and Karma, so you can understand how it fits into Vedic astrology and the lunar nodes.

What Is Sidereal Astrology?

Western horoscopes use tropical astrology, but we mustn't forget about true sidereal astrology. Both types involve signs named after constellations, but there is one significant difference: tropical astrology is based on a map of the stars in the exact positions they were in 0 AD, while Sidereal astrology is based on the position of the constellations at the time of the reading.

The stars move over time, which changes their position relative to Earth; this means that there is a 24-degree difference between the constellations and the tropical map. You would likely have two different sun signs if you checked both systems.

Here are the birth dates for both astrological systems.

SIGN	SIDEREAL	TROPICAL
Aries	April 21 - May 12	March 21 - April 19
Taurus	May 13 - June 19	April 20 - May 20
Gemini	June 20 - July 16	May 21 - June 20
Cancer	July 17 - August 6	June 21 - July 22
Leo	August 7 - September 14	July 23 - August 22
Virgo	September 15 - November 3	August 23 - September 22

SIGN	SIDEREAL	TROPICAL
Libra	November 4 - November 22	September 23 - October 22
Scorpio	November 23 - December 6	October 23 - November 21
Ophiuchus	December 7 - December 18	
Sagittarius	December 19 - January 19	November 22 - December 21
Capricorn	January 20 - February 13	December 22 - January 19
Aquarius	February 14 - March 9	January 20 - February 19
Pisces	March 10 - April 20	February 20 - March 20

If your birth date falls three days before or after your sign change, you are considered to be on the cusp.

Ancient cultures used the Sidereal system because it was (and still is) an easier way to interpret the stars to see how they were at any given time in the past. Sidereal astrology has its foundations in the birth time and place of an individual and what was happening in the sky at the time; by contrast, the tropical system is considered theoretical and linked to the seasons on Earth.

You will understand more about all this as you work through this book. The next chapter delves into the Navagrahas.

Chapter 2: What Are the Navagrahas?

According to ancient Hindu texts such as the Brahma-Siddhanta and Yavana-jataka, Navagraha refers to the nine planets with significant influence in Vedic Astrology. These planets are thought to significantly impact human life, shaping individual lives and destinies and influencing certain aspects of an individual's existence.

Navagrahas are deities according to Vedic astrology.
Daderot, CC0, via Wikimedia Commons:
https://commons.wikimedia.org/wiki/File:Navagraha_(anthropomorphic_forms_of_astronomical_bodies),_Bihar,_India,_10th_century_AD,_schist_-_San_Diego_Museum_of_Art_-_DSC06389.JPG

The concept of Navagraha acknowledges that the nine planets are cosmic forces with immense power that they exert over all human life. In order, they are:

- Surya – the Sun
- Chandra – the Moon
- Mangala – Mars
- Budha – Mercury
- Guru/Brihaspati – Jupiter
- Shukra – Venus
- Shani – Saturn
- Rahu – North Node
- Ketu – South Node

Each one represents a specific planetary energy and has a certain mythological significance.

According to Vedic astrology, the Navagrahas are deities. They are revered for their influence over humans, including mental and physical wellbeing, wealth, careers, relationships, and spiritual growth. Where the planets are positioned and their alignment at the exact time of an individual's birth is mapped onto a chart known as the Janam Kundli or a birth chart or horoscope. By analyzing these positions, an astrologer gains insight into the individual's life events, personality traits, and future potential.

Rahu and Ketu are not considered gods. Rather, they are the Moon's shadow nodes, demons who used their smarts to grab a place in astrology, and their names originate from shady, hostile planets in the solar system – Neptune and Pluto.

The Navagrahas

The Sun – Lord Surya

The Sun god, Lord Surya, or Ravi, is located dead center of the solar system, surrounded by the remaining planets. The Sun always faces East, while the other planets face other directions but never face one another.

Hindu mythology tells us that Surya rides the sky on a golden chariot pulled by seven horses. That number is significant, representing the colors in the rainbow, the chakras, the days of the week, and anything else that comes in sevens. He is depicted with four arms and holds a mace and lotus flowers. As he travels, he moves through each zodiac sign and spends around a month in each.

Surya represents intelligence, vitality, and leadership and is associated with self-confidence, power, and authority.

The Moon – Lord Chandra

Also known as Soma, Chandra is depicted as a beautiful deity, but as the moon waxes and wanes, he is rarely shown whole. He wears white clothing and holds a lotus flower and a club. He represents intuition, emotion, and the mind and governs emotional wellbeing, moods, and the subconscious. Chandra is also associated with feminine energy, creativity, and nurturing.

Chandra travels in a chariot drawn by 10 horses and moves faster than the sun, spending around 2 ½ days in each zodiac sign.

Mars – Mangala

Mangala also goes by *Angaraka* and is depicted as a fearsome god with four hands holding a mace, trident, spear, and lotus flower. It is believed he is the offspring of Bhumi, the goddess of Earth, or Privthi. He is associated with ambition, passion, and pursuing goals and represents drive, assertiveness, and physical strength.

He travels in a chariot drawn by eight red horses or on a ram and spends about four days to several months in each zodiac sign.

Mercury – Budha

Budha is considered the offspring of Lord Chandra and is typically depicted as a young god with four hands holding a shield, sword, and lotus flower. He represents wit, speech, and learning, and, as the planet of commerce, communication, and intellect, he governs analytical thinking, intelligence, and adaptability.

Budha travels on a lion or chariot and moves quite quickly through the solar system, spending around 14 to 30 days in each zodiac sign.

Jupiter – Brihaspati

Jupiter is the planet of knowledge, wisdom, and expansion, also known as Guru, the teacher of gods. He is associated with generosity, abundance, and higher learning, symbolizing growth, spirituality, and good fortune.

Jupiter is usually depicted as wise and benevolent, with four arms and holding prayer beads, a lotus flower, a staff, and a water container. He rides a chariot with eight horses or a lotus flower and moves slowly, spending about a year in each zodiac sign.

Venus – Shukra

Shukra is depicted as a handsome god but is considered an instructor of demons. He represents relationships, beauty, and love and governs artistic expression, harmony, and romance. Associated with material comfort, luxury, and pleasure, Shukra is typically shown with four arms holding a water container, lotus flower, mirror, and staff. He rides a lotus flower or a chariot with eight horses and moves through the solar system at a moderate pace, often staying in each zodiac sign for about a month.

Saturn – Shani

Saturn is considered the planet of hard work, responsibility, and discipline but is a stormy god who can build and destroy good fortune, depending on where he is in the solar system at any given time. He also represents karma, life lessons, and maturity and is associated with pursuing long-term goals, perseverance, and endurance. He is typically depicted as dark and muscular, holding a club, bow, arrows, and a sword, and travels in a chariot drawn by eight black horses. He travels slowly through the solar system, staying in each zodiac sign for around 2 ½ years.

Rahu

Rahu is the Moon's North node and is considered to be a demon rather than a god. He is a shadow planet signifying desires, ambitions, and worldly pursuits and represents materialism, unconventional thinking, and a craving for success. He represents challenges and opportunities and is typically depicted as a serpent-like figure with the head of a dragon and long sharp teeth. He travels on a throne or chariot, and because he is a shadow planet, Rahu has no physical existence. His movements are closely tied to how the lunar nodes are aligned with the Moon and Sun.

Ketu

The Moon's South node, Ketu, is the second shadow planet and is associated with liberation, spirituality, and enlightenment. He represents detachment, introspection, and mystical experiences and typically signifies karmic lessons. He is also depicted as serpent-like but without a head and travels on a throne or chariot. Again, as a shadow planet, Ketu doesn't have a physical existence, and his movement is connected to alignment with the Moon and Sun.

Interpretations and Traits

Here's an overview of each planet in Vedic astrology, showing their interpretations, traits, interactions, and life aspects:

The Sun
Interpretation:
- Authority
- Ego
- Father
- Government
- Power
- Self
- Vitality

Positive Traits:
- Confidence
- Generosity
- Intelligence
- Willpower

Negative Traits:
- Arrogance
- Dominance
- Stubbornness

Interactions:
- Harmony – Mars and Jupiter
- Conflicts – Venus and Saturn

Aspects of Life:
- Career
- Fatherly influence
- Leadership
- Success

The Moon
Interpretation:
- Emotions

- Fertility
- Intuition
- Mind
- Mother
- Nurturing

Positive Traits:
- Adaptability
- Compassion
- Creativity
- Sensitivity

Negative Traits:
- Emotional instability
- Moods
- Over-sensitivity

Interactions:
- Harmony – Venus and Jupiter
- Conflict – Ketu and Rahu

Aspects of Life:
- Creativity
- Emotions
- Intuition
- Relationships

Mars

Interpretation:
- Aggression
- Courage
- Energy
- Passion
- Physical strength

Positive Traits:
- Determination
- Ambition

- Confidence
- Resilience

Negative Traits:
- Aggression
- Anger
- Impulsiveness

Interactions:
- Harmony – Jupiter and the Sun
- Conflict – Saturn and Mercury

Aspects of Life:
- Conflict resolution
- Courage
- Courage
- Physical strength

Mercury

Interpretation:
- Commerce
- Communication
- Intellect
- Learning
- Logic

Positive Traits:
- Analytical skills
- Intelligence
- Versatility
- Wit

Negative Traits:
- Indecisiveness
- Nervousness
- Restlessness

Interactions:
- Harmony – Saturn and Venus

- Conflict – the Moon and Mars

Jupiter
Interpretation:
- Expansion
- Good fortune
- Knowledge
- Spirituality
- Wisdom

Positive Traits:
- Generosity
- Growth
- Optimism
- Wisdom

Negative Traits:
- Excessive optimism
- Overindulgence
- Self-righteousness

Interactions:
- Harmony – the Sun and Moon
- Conflict – Venus and Mercury

Aspects of Life:
- Expansion
- Good fortune
- Spirituality
- Wisdom

Venus
Interpretation:
- Art
- Beauty
- Harmony
- Love
- Material comfort

- Relationships

Positive Traits:
- Charm
- Creativity
- Diplomacy
- Romance

Negative Traits:
- Indulgence
- Superficiality
- Vanity

Interactions:
- Harmony – Saturn and Mercury
- Conflict – Jupiter and Mars

Aspects of Life:
- Beauty
- Creativity
- Love
- Material comfort
- Relationships

Saturn

Interpretation:
- Discipline
- Hard work
- Karma
- Life lessons
- Responsibility

Positive Traits:
- Discipline
- Patience
- Perseverance
- Practicality

Negative Traits:
- Pessimism
- Restriction
- Rigidity

Interactions:
- Harmony – Mercury and Venus
- Conflict – the Moon and Sun

Aspects of Life:
- Discipline
- Hard work
- Karmic influence
- Life lessons

Rahu
Interpretations:
- Ambition
- Desires
- Illusion
- Obsession
- Worldly pursuits

Positive Traits:
- Ambition
- Innovation
- Unconventional thinking

Negative Traits:
- Deception
- Obsession
- Restlessness

Interactions:
- Harmony – Mercury and Saturn
- Conflict – Mars and Jupiter

Aspects of Life:
- Ambition

- Desires
- Spiritual growth
- Worldly pursuits

Ketu
Interactions:
- Detachment
- Karmic lessons
- Liberation
- Mysticism
- Spirituality

Positive Traits:
- Detachment
- Introspection
- Spiritual growth

Negative Traits:
- Confusion
- Detachment from worldly matters
- Escapism

Interactions:
- Harmony – Jupiter and Mars
- Conflict – the Sun and Moon

Aspects of Life:
- Karmic lessons
- Liberation
- Spiritual growth

While based on the traditional beliefs and principles of Vedic astrology, these interpretations are subject to change based on their position and aspects in each person's birth chart, which can lead to different influences and manifestations.

Planetary Associations

And now, an overview of each planet's associations:

Surya - Sun:
- **Horoscope:** Leo (Simha)
- **Day:** Sunday (Ravivar)
- **Number:** 1
- **Color:** Red
- **Gemstone:** Ruby
- **Overseer Deity:** Lord Shiva
- **Protects:** heart, head, eyes, bones

Chandra - Moon:
- **Horoscope:** Cancer (Karka)
- **Day:** Monday (Somvar)
- **Number:** 2
- **Color:** White
- **Gemstone:** Pearl
- **Overseer Deity:** Goddess Parvati
- **Protects:** mind, brain, right eye (women), left eye (men)

Mangala - Mars:
- **Horoscope:** Aries (Mesha) and Scorpio (Vrishchika)
- **Day:** Tuesday (Mangalvar)
- **Number:** 9
- **Color:** Red
- **Gemstone:** Coral
- **Overseer Deity:** Lord Murugan
- **Protects:** muscles, head, blood

Budha - Mercury:
- **Horoscope:** Gemini (Mithuna) and Virgo (Kanya)
- **Day:** Wednesday (Budhvar)
- **Number:** 5
- **Color:** Green
- **Gemstone:** Emerald

- **Overseer Deity**: Lord Vishnu
- **Protects**: skin, speech organs, nervous system

Guru - Jupiter:
- **Horoscope**: Sagittarius (Dhanu) and Pisces (Meena)
- **Day**: Thursday (Guruvar)
- **Number**: 3
- **Color**: Yellow
- **Gemstone**: Yellow Sapphire
- **Overseer Deity**: Lord Brahma
- **Protects**: liver, thighs, stomach

Shukra - Venus:
- **Horoscope**: Taurus (Vrishabha) and Libra (Tula)
- **Day**: Friday (Shukravar)
- **Number**: 6
- **Color**: White
- **Gemstone**: Diamond
- **Overseer Deity**: Goddess Lakshmi
- **Protects**: throat, urinary system, reproductive organs

Shani - Saturn:
- **Horoscope**: Capricorn (Makara) and Aquarius (Kumbha)
- **Day**: Saturday (Shanivar)
- **Number**: 8
- **Color**: Black
- **Gemstone**: Blue Sapphire
- **Overseer Deity**: Lord Yama
- **Protects**: nervous system, bones, teeth, knees

Rahu - North Node of the Moon:
- **Horoscope**: Not associated with any specific horoscope
- **Day**: No specific day
- **Number**: 4
- **Color**: Smoky
- **Gemstone**: Hessonite Garnet

- **Overseer Deity**: Goddess Durga
- **Protects**: thighs, limbs, phlegm

Ketu - South Node of the Moon:
- **Horoscope**: Not associated with any specific horoscope
- **Day**: No specific day
- **Number**: 7
- **Color**: Transparent
- **Gemstone**: Cat's Eye
- **Overseer Deity**: Lord Ganesha
- **Protects**: feet, ears, and digestive system

Chapter 3: What Are the Lunar Nodes?

The lunar nodes are sometimes called the Nodes of Fate or the Nodes of Destiny. They are not physical; they are invisible points in the sky where the Sun and the Moon's paths cross, which happens several times a year. Do you know when it is? It's when the Earth experiences an eclipse.

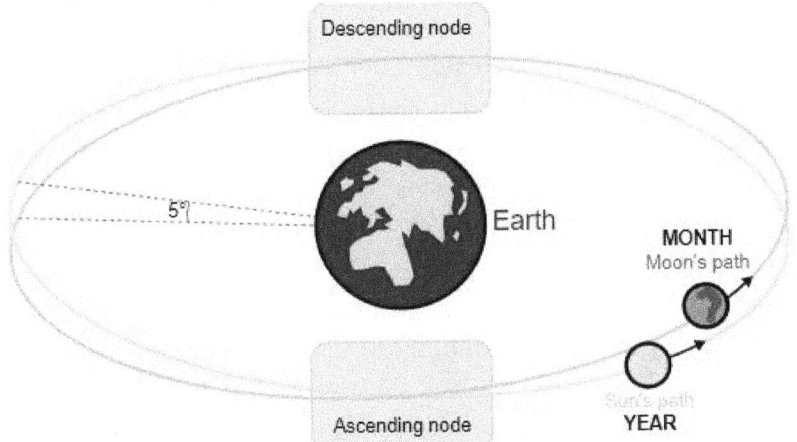

Lunar nodes are invisible points in the sky when the sun and moon's paths cross.
https://commons.wikimedia.org/wiki/File:Lunar_eclipse_diagram-it.svg

The nodes tell you the spiritual path you should be aiming for. They also tell you which paths you should get off and leave behind and what type of energy you are working with at the time of the reading. In astrology, the moon has two shadow nodes – the North and South nodes.

The North node is about the here and now and the future, and the South is about the past. Every 18 months, the nodes will change signs but always be in opposite signs, i.e., when the North node enters Leo, the South node enters Aquarius.

These nodes also inform you what happens to you when an eclipse occurs based on the modes in your birth charts and the transiting nodes.

Vedic astrology has distinct names for these lunar nodes - Rahu and Ketu. It's a long story about how it all came about, but to keep things short and to the point, a demon made the gods agree to him being immortal. However, he was not meant to have the power of immortality, and his tricks angered the gods. To punish him, they gave him immortality but with a nasty twist: he would forever be part past, which is Ketu, and part future, which is Rahu; as such, he would never be able to get away from himself or his evil deeds.

Let's take a deeper look at the lunar nodes.

The North Node

The North node, otherwise called Rahu, tells us where we are going; we are stepping into the unknown, a place we don't know anything about, almost like you have moved to a new city, don't know anyone, and are starting over. This is a time for you to be who you want to be, put your past behind you, and reinvent yourself.

The energy from the North node allows you to reinvent your life and world. How you use that energy is entirely up to you, but using these powers for good things is important.

Positive Traits

In Vedic astrology, the North node is representative of life lessons, the point of growth, and the potential in your birth chart. It has several positive traits, but these will vary depending on the positions of the houses and signs. Some of the general positive traits are:

- **Life Purpose:** Rahu indicates your purpose in life and the direction you should be heading for. If you embrace this path wholeheartedly, it will bring you a sense of growth and personal fulfillment.
- **Soul Growth:** Rahu represents the experiences and lessons your soul wants to learn and integrate into your present life. When you embrace these lessons, you will experience spiritual and

personal development.
- **New Opportunities:** Rahu signifies opportunity and growth possibilities, encouraging you to leave your comfort zone and head into the unknown.
- **Positive Traits You Should Develop:** Rahu indicates the positive qualities you should focus on cultivating and expressing. It encourages the development and embodiment of those specific traits so that you can achieve interpersonal and personal success.
- **Karmic Release:** When you focus on the lessons Rahu brings, your karmic patterns can be released, and you can overcome the challenges you allowed to hold you back previously.
- **Relationship and Collaboration Skills:** Rahu typically places great emphasis on cooperation and healthy relationships, encouraging stronger interpersonal skills, building good connections, and encouraging teamwork.
- **Personal Empowerment:** When you embrace Rahu's energy, you can benefit from more self-confidence, better personal identity, and more self-empowerment.

Don't forget; Rahu's positive traits are entirely dependent on your zodiac sign and where the houses are positioned in your birth chart.

Career and Professional Development

The North Node has a significant role to play in your career and professional development. It represents the lessons you should pursue and the direction you should go to fulfill your purpose in life and achieve good personal growth. Here's how Rahu influences you in these areas:

- **Career Path:** Rahu gives you significant insight into the right career path to align with your purpose in life. It can tell you what kind of career you should be looking for to be fulfilled and happy.
- **New Opportunities:** Rahu brings new experiences and opportunities that help you forge ahead in your career, encouraging you to leave your comfort zone and explore new things.
- **Embracing New Challenges:** Rahu may provide lessons and challenges related to your career. If you face these challenges head-on, you can develop the qualities and skills you need to succeed professionally.

- **Developing Skills:** Rahu highlights certain qualities or skills to help you develop in your career, encouraging you to get the expertise you need to achieve your goals and focus on personal growth.
- **Collaborative Ventures:** Rahu will often emphasize how important teamwork and collaboration are in your professional life. Rahu encourages you to make the right partnerships and create positive relationships with your mentors and colleagues to help your career grow.
- **Reputation and Public Image:** Rahu may influence how others in your professional arena perceive you. It provides encouragement in cultivating the reputation and public image needed to align with your values and purpose in life.
- **Finding Fulfillment:** If you follow Rahu's guidance, you will be satisfied and fulfilled in your professional life. When your professional pursuits align with your life purpose, you will experience contentment and meaning in your work.

How to Identify and Fulfill The North Node's Energy

To identify the North Node's energy and fulfill it in your birth chart, you need to learn self-reflection and awareness and be conscious of your actions in alignment with Rahu's lessons. Some ways to identify and fulfill the North Node's energy are:

- **Studying Your Birth Chart:** Look at your birth chart to identify your North Node's house placement and zodiac sign. When you can understand the themes and characteristics of the house and sign, you gain good insight into your North Node's lessons and energy.
- **Reflect on Past Patterns:** Think about patterns and experiences in your life that seem to have stagnated or keep repeating. The South Node, which you'll learn about shortly, is the opposite of the North Node, representing familiarity and comfort zones. Reflect on whether those patterns and experiences align with your North Node's energy and lessons or whether they have held you back and stopped you from growing.
- **Awareness and Self-Reflection:** Learn to self-reflect and identify areas where you may be fighting against the North Node's energy. Look deep at your fears, motivations, and desires to be aware of behaviors and patterns holding you back.

- **Embrace New Experiences**: Rahu tends to encourage people to leave their comfort zone and explore new territory. Be open to new experiences, explore where you've never been, and take risks as long as they align with your North Node's energy.
- **Develop New Qualities and Skills**: Identify the qualities, skills, and traits associated with your North Node's house placement and zodiac. Be proactive in developing and embodying those qualities in your personal and professional life, and look for opportunities where you can grow. Invest in new experiences that align with the energy from your North Node.
- **Set Goals and Intentions**: When you set them, be specific and make sure they align with your North Node's energy. They can be to do with your career, personal development, relationships, or anything else. When you create a roadmap, you can focus on that energy and move towards fulfilling it.
- **Get Guidance**: Seek advice from a specialist life coach or astrologer, as they can give you great insight and specific guidance on the placement of your North Node. This helps you understand its energy and fulfill it.

It's important to remember that the energy of your North Node is a journey for life, and progress will likely be slow. Be patient; let personal growth and lessons come naturally. When you embrace your North Node's energy, you will experience fulfillment, better self-awareness, and more attuned to your life's purpose.

The South Node

Better known as Ketu, the South node keeps a record of every past life you have lived; it records where you have been, your energies, emotions, and relationships. This is the Karmic energy you want to leave behind as you live your current life. This is where your sense of déjà vu comes from, the feeling that something is familiar, and that's because you've likely already been there in a past life. It also shows you feelings and patterns you bring from the past to your present life, and while something might not be happening, it is something you hold onto. It's important to leave sentiments like this behind, but that's not easy because if you don't remain super-conscious and aware of what you are doing, you can easily slip back into old habits.

Negative Traits

The South Node represents past patterns, comfort zone, and all our Karmic baggage. That's not to say it's a negative node. However, relying on it too much or overemphasizing it may manifest as negative traits or challenges. Some of the South Node's potential negative traits are:

1. **Resisting Change and Stagnating:** Ketu symbolizes a common tendency among humans – to resist change and hang on to old, familiar patterns. This indicates a reluctance to try anything new and to leave your comfort zone, which can seriously hinder evolution and personal growth.
2. **Repeating Unhealthy Patterns:** Ketu also symbolizes past patterns, particularly repetitive ones, including attitudes, behaviors, or certain dynamics in relationships that don't serve you in your personal growth. These are likely to keep you trapped in unhealthy and unproductive cycles.
3. **Too Dependent on Familiarity:** Too much reliance on things or feelings that are familiar and comfortable can lead to missed growth opportunities and a fear of the unknown. This can stop you from looking for new opportunities and possibilities.
4. **Resisting Progress:** Ketu's energy is sometimes exhibited as a lack of motivation to move forward, and this can result in you resisting change and not wanting to advance yourself personally or professionally by taking risks.
5. **Hanging onto the Past:** Ketu indicates that you may prefer to stay in the past, hanging on to regrets, hurts, and nostalgia. Being fixated on the past can stop you from embracing your present life and self and creating your desired future.
6. **Struggling to Let Go:** Ketu suggests that you may struggle to let go of relationships, attachments, or situations that don't serve your personal growth. This can stop you from progressing and trap you in a never-ending cycle of old situations.
7. **Repressing Rahu's Lessons:** If your South Node energy is overly dominant, it suggests you are resisting or even avoiding the North Node's lessons and the growth it can bring. This means you miss opportunities to develop personally and spiritually.

Remember that everyone has a unique birth chart, and the South Node's negative traits depend entirely on its house placement and zodiac sign. Awareness of the challenges can help you work consciously toward balancing the South Node's energy with the North Node's positive qualities to ensure the best environment for evolution and personal growth.

How the South Node Represents Your Past Life Karma

As far as astrology goes, the South Node is strongly associated with past-life Karma, all the experiences and lessons from your past lives that never got resolved. The following show you how Ketu could potentially represent your past-life Karma:

- **Karmic Baggage:** Ketu symbolizes all your unresolved issues, patterns, and experiences from past lives. It represents the tendencies you may default to or the comfort zone you are used to because of how you were conditioned in your past lives.

- **Familiar Habits and Patterns:** Ketu reflects deeply ingrained habits, behaviors, and beliefs because of peated experiences in your past lives. These could be negative and positive patterns, all shaping your present-life tendencies and responses.

- **Learning and Resolving Lessons:** Ketu indicates all the challenges and Karmic lessons you brought from past lives into the present so you can address them and find a solution. It represents where in your life you may find yourself repeating specific patterns or experiences or stumbling over obstacles until you have learned the lessons intended for you.

- **Attachment and Over-Identification:** Ketu indicates that you might over-identify with attachments, identities, or roles from your past lives. This kind of attachment can stop you from creating new experiences for yourself and stopping your personal growth. It stops you from embracing your present life fully.

- **Patterns to Transcend:** the South Node's negative traits may represent specific patterns you must transcend to evolve and spiritually progress. While these patterns may have been useful in past lives, they no longer serve your development and growth.

- **Balancing the North and South Nodes:** these two opposite points represent your growth direction and the lessons you need to learn in your present life. The ability to balance their energy is critical if you are to integrate all your past-life Karma and move forward on your life's path.

Past-life Karma is a subjective concept, and not everyone accepts it. How the South Node is interpreted as past-life Karma is based entirely on specific beliefs, both spiritual and philosophical. Suppose the idea of past-life Karma resonates with you. In that case, you will find it useful to explore your South Node's challenges and lessons, as they can give you some useful insights into certain unresolved areas of your soul's journey.

The South Node and Spiritual Development

Ketu has a big role to play in spiritual development; while it is typically linked to Karmic baggage and past patterns, the South Node also provides some great opportunities for you to transform yourself and grow on your spiritual path. Spiritual development is influenced in the following ways:

- **Karmic Lessons:** Ketu represents unresolved issues from your past life. Understanding those lessons and understanding them is a good way to gain insight into the journey your soul is on. It also shows you where you need to grow and heal to develop spiritually.
- **Breaking Away from Patterns:** Ketu highlights behaviors and patterns that don't contribute to your spiritual development. When you can recognize them, you can work consciously to break away from them, a critical part of your spiritual evolution.
- **Let Go:** Ketu extends an invitation to you; it asks you to let go of attachments, relationships, or beliefs that no longer serve you and just get in the way of your spiritual development. When you can release what you no longer need, you gain the space you need to enjoy higher vibrations and new experiences.
- **Balance the Nodes:** you must learn to balance the North and South Node's energy if you are to develop spiritually. The North Node maps out your personal growth and purpose in life, while the South Node provides lessons from past lives, and balancing the two can help you evolve.
- **Transcend Your Ego Attachments:** Ketu's influence can highlight any attachments and tendencies driven by your ego that get in the way of spiritual development. It allows you to transcend those identifications and learn to build and embrace other qualities, such as non-attachment, surrender, and humility.
- **Healing and Integration:** Ketu's energy provides you with the opportunities you need to heal unresolved emotions and wounds from past lives and integrate them into your present life. When

you can acknowledge and work through these challenges, those blockages will clear, and your spiritual path will be more harmonious and open.

- **Soul Evotion:** the lessons your South Node teaches you to contribute to how your soul evolves. When you can embrace the opportunities, Ketu provides for growth, your spiritual development can accelerate and be better aligned with your higher, spiritual self.

The South Node's energy must be approached with a self-reflective, compassionate, and fully aware mindset. Everyone has their own spiritual journey, and the South Node offers each one of us unique lessons for transformation and growth. When you take part in certain practices, such as energy healing, self-inquiry, meditation, and asking spiritual teachers for guidance, your exploration of Ketu during your spiritual development is fully supported.

How to Find the North and South Nodes

To find the North and South nodes in Vedic astrology requires you to work out their positions based on your birth chart. The following steps will help you work out your node placements:

1. **Get Your Birth Chart:** to do this, you need to know the exact time, date, and place of your birth – more about this later in the guide.
2. **Locate the Lagna (Ascendant):** the Ascendant in Vedic astrology is the birth chart's starting point, representing the rising sign when you were born. You will need the Ascendant's sign and degree.
3. **Identify the Moon's Position:** you need to find the Moon's sign and degree in your birth chart. Where the Moon is placed is critical for determining where Rahu and Ketu are located.
4. **Calculate the Position of Rahu:** in your birth chart, Rahu is always directly opposite the Moon.
5. **Calculate the Position of Ketu:** Ketu will always be directly opposite Rahu, which means it shares the Moon's degree and sign.

When you know their positions, you can begin to learn their significance in Vedic astrology and interpret their effects on you and others. Rahu is associated with ambition, material pursuits, worldly attachment, and desires. Ketu is associated with detachment, spiritual growth, liberation, and karmic lessons.

Rahu-Ketu Date Ranges

Below you can find the approximate date ranges for Rahu and Ketu in the zodiac signs:

Aries – Mesha
North Node
- February 12, 1942 - August 12, 1943
- September 2, 1960 - March 25, 1962
- April 13, 1979 - October 12, 1980
- November 4, 1997 - April 20, 1999
- May 9, 2016 - November 6, 2017

South Node
- February 12, 1942 - August 12, 1943
- September 2, 1960 - March 25, 1962
- April 13, 1979 - October 12, 1980
- November 4, 1997 - April 20, 1999
- May 9, 2016 - November 6, 2017

Taurus – Vrishabha
North Node
- August 13, 1943 - February 11, 1945
- March 26, 1962 - September 19, 1963
- October 13, 1980 - April 5, 1982
- April 21, 1999 - November 7, 2000
- November 7, 2017 - March 22, 2019

South Node
- August 13, 1943 - February 11, 1945
- March 26, 1962 - September 19, 1963
- October 13, 1980 - April 5, 1982
- April 21, 1999 - November 7, 2000
- November 7, 2017 - March 22, 2019

Gemini – Mithuna
North Node
- February 12, 1945 - August 11, 1946

- September 20, 1963 - March 17, 1965
- April 6, 1982 - December 1, 1983
- November 7, 2000 - April 13, 2002
- March 23, 2019 - September 19, 2020

South Node
- February 12, 1945 - August 11, 1946
- September 20, 1963 - March 17, 1965
- April 6, 1982 - December 1, 1983
- November 7, 2000 - April 13, 2002
- March 23, 2019 - September 19, 2020

Cancer – Karka
North Node
- August 12, 1946 - February 11, 1948
- March 18, 1965 - September 11, 1966
- December 2, 1983 - May 21, 1985
- April 14, 2002 - October 13, 2003
- September 20, 2020 - March 16, 2022

South Node
- August 12, 1946 - February 11, 1948
- March 18, 1965 - September 11, 1966
- December 2, 1983 - May 21, 1985
- April 14, 2002 - October 13, 2003
- September 20, 2020 - March 16, 2022.

Leo – Simha
North Node
- February 12, 1948 - August 11, 1949
- September 12, 1966 - March 7, 1968
- May 22, 1985 - December 19, 1986
- October 14, 2003 - April 13, 2005
- March 17, 2022 - September 11, 2023

South Node
- February 12, 1948 - August 11, 1949

- September 12, 1966 - March 7, 1968
- May 22, 1985 - December 19, 1986
- October 14, 2003 - April 13, 2005
- March 17, 2022 - September 11, 2023.

Virgo - Kanya
North Node
- August 12, 1949 - February 11, 1951
- March 8, 1968 - August 2, 1969
- December 20, 1986 - June 19, 1988
- April 14, 2005 - October 13, 2006
- September 12, 2023 - May 4, 2025

South Node
- August 12, 1949 - February 11, 1951
- March 8, 1968 - August 2, 1969
- December 20, 1986 - June 19, 1988
- April 14, 2005 - October 13, 2006
- September 12, 2023 - May 4, 2025

Libra - Tula
North Node
- February 12, 1951 - August 11, 1952
- August 3, 1969 - January 27, 1971
- June 20, 1988 - December 12, 1989
- October 14, 2006 - April 13, 2008
- May 5, 2025 - November 1, 2026

South Node
- February 12, 1951 - August 11, 1952
- August 3, 1969 - January 27, 1971
- June 20, 1988 - December 12, 1989
- October 14, 2006 - April 13, 2008
- May 5, 2025 - November 1, 2026

Scorpio - Vrishchika
North Node
- August 12, 1952 - February 11, 1954
- January 28, 1971 - July 25, 1972
- December 13, 1989 - June 9, 1991
- April 14, 2008 - October 13, 2009
- November 2, 2026 - April 19, 2028

South Node
- August 12, 1952 - February 11, 1954
- January 28, 1971 - July 25, 1972
- December 13, 1989 - June 9, 1991
- April 14, 2008 - October 13, 2009
- November 2, 2026 - April 19, 2028

Sagittarius - Dhanu
North Node
- February 12, 1954 - August 11, 1955
- July 26, 1972 - January 22, 1974
- June 10, 1991 - December 3, 1992
- October 14, 2009 - April 12, 2011
- April 20, 2028 - November 16, 2029

South Node
- February 12, 1954 - August 11, 1955
- July 26, 1972 - January 22, 1974
- June 10, 1991 - December 3, 1992
- October 14, 2009 - April 12, 2011
- April 20, 2028 - November 16, 2029

Capricorn - Makara
North Node
- August 12, 1955 - February 11, 1957
- January 23, 1974 - July 16, 1975
- December 4, 1992 - June 30, 1994
- April 13, 2011 - October 12, 2012

- November 17, 2029 - May 14, 2031

South Node
- August 12, 1955 - February 11, 1957
- January 23, 1974 - July 16, 1975
- December 4, 1992 - June 30, 1994
- April 13, 2011 - October 12, 2012
- November 17, 2029 - May 14, 2031

Aquarius - Kumbha
North Node
- February 12, 1957 - August 11, 1958
- July 17, 1975 - January 12, 1977
- July 1, 1994 - December 28, 1995
- October 13, 2012 - April 12, 2014
- May 15, 2031 - November 11, 2032

South Node
- February 12, 1957 - August 11, 1958
- July 17, 1975 - January 12, 1977
- July 1, 1994 - December 28, 1995
- October 13, 2012 - April 12, 2014
- May 15, 2031 - November 11, 2032

Pisces - Meena
North Node
- August 12, 1958 - February 11, 1960
- January 13, 1977 - July 9, 1978
- December 29, 1995 - June 23, 1997
- April 13, 2014 - October 13, 2015
- November 12, 2032 - May 9, 2034

South Node
- August 12, 1958 - February 11, 1960
- January 13, 1977 - July 9, 1978
- December 29, 1995 - June 23, 1997
- April 13, 2014 - October 13, 2015

- November 12, 2032 - May 9, 2034

Please note these date ranges are a general guideline only and may vary slightly depending on what calculations are used in Vedic astrology.

Note that the South Node will always be the same degree as the opposite sign in the North Node:
- Aries North/Libra South
- Taurus North/Scorpio South
- Gemini North/Sagittarius South
- Cancer North/Capricorn South
- Leo North/Aquarius South
- Virgo North/Pisces South
- Libra North/Aries South
- Scorpio North/Taurus South
- Sagittarius North/Gemini South
- Capricorn North/Cancer South
- Aquarius North/Leo South
- Pisces North/Virgo South

The Nodes in the Houses:

On your birth chart, the North and South nodes are represented by glyphs:
- North Node (Rahu): ☊
- South Node (Ketu): ☋

Look at your kundli and find the symbols; mark them. When you find one, the other will be in an opposite sign and house, but they will both be at the same degree. When you know what house they are in on your birth chart, you better understand your Karma and energy. Here's an overview:

The First House:
- **Rahu:** brings a desire for self-expression, recognition, and personal identity and has the potential to create an ambitious, charismatic personality.
- **Ketu:** allows you to focus spiritually on self-realization and brings introspection and detachment from the material world.

The Second House:
- **Rahu:** brings a drive for material security, possessions, and wealth, strengthens communication skills, and enhances a sense of self-worth.
- **Ketu:** allows your focus to be on your spiritual values, brings about detachment from wealth (materially speaking), and a need to go beyond the material realm and explore deeper truths.

The Third House:
- **Rahu:** focuses on intellectual pursuits, strengthening communication, ambition, and courage. It also encourages a need for recognition using networking and other skills.
- **Ketu:** detaches you from insignificant social interactions, makes you want to explore spiritual knowledge, and makes you tend toward introspection.

The Fourth House:
- **Rahu:** brings a need for family, home, and emotional security. It also makes you want recognition and success in domestic matters.
- **Ketu:** makes you move away from emotional attachment, focus on your inner wisdom and growth, and gives a need for solitude, spiritually speaking.

The Fifth House:
- **Rahu:** enhances intelligence and creativity and brings a need for fame and self-expression. It can also make you want to strive for enjoyment and personal desire.
- **Ketu:** makes you move away from desires driven by your ego and encourages selfless service and creativity to enhance spiritual growth while also looking for a deeper meaning in your life.

The Sixth House:
- **Rahu:** encourages competitiveness, ambition, and a need for success to help you overcome enemies and challenges. It may also strengthen your problem-solving skills and encourage you to focus on improving yourself.
- **Ketu:** makes you move away from worldly conflict, focus your attention on spiritual service and healing, and a desire to liberate yourself spiritually from obstacles.

The Seventh House:
- **Rahu:** brings a desire for social connections, partnerships, and relationships and can enhance a drive to make partnerships successful and strengthen charisma.
- **Ketu:** makes you stop being overly dependent on a relationship, makes you want your relationships to bring spiritual growth, and puts your focus on inner harmony.

The Eight House:
- **Rahu:** allows you to learn more from transformative experiences and your knowledge of the occult and creates a desire to learn more about the unknown and gain spiritual transformation.
- **Ketu:** makes you move away from an attachment to material things, creates a lean towards the spiritual, and a need to be liberated from Karmic patterns.

The Ninth House:
- **Rahu:** creates a desire for spirituality, higher knowledge, and pursuits of the philosophical type. It may also create stronger spiritual growth and a drive to explore and go on long-distance journeys.
- **Ketu:** makes you move away from belief and dogma, lean towards spirituality, and crave higher truth and inner wisdom.

The Tenth House:
- **Rahu:** creates stronger career aspirations, ambition, and a need for recognition and social status. It may also bring about a need for professional leadership and success.
- **Ketu:** makes you move away from worldly achievements, want to find a deep sense of purpose, and focus more on inner growth, spiritually speaking.

The Eleventh House:
- **Rahu:** makes you crave material gains, social networks, and connections. It might also strengthen your ambition and drive to achieve your goals successfully.
- **Ketu:** makes you want to detach from material desires, brings a need for inner fulfillment that goes beyond what your achievements bring you, and a focus on collective consciousness and spiritual friendships.

The Twelfth House:
- **Rahu:** enhances your sense of solitude and spiritual experiences and makes you want to be liberated from worldly attachments. You may also become fascinated with a need for self-realization.
- **Ketu:** makes you want to walk away from material illusions, gain inner enlightenment and peace, and focus more on becoming spiritually liberated.

The influence each node has will depend on the birth chart and its different factors, including the aspects of each planet and any conjunctions.

North Node Planets

Planets commonly align with the North and South nodes in an individual's birth chart, but it isn't a given, so if none align with yours, don't worry about it.

While the North node planets reveal your current and future life energy, the South node planets are all about the energy that ran through your past lives: North tells you what comes from the past lives, and South tells you what you left back there. Let's say your kundli shows the Sun in the South node. That means you are working hard to move on from an insecure past life. If it's in the North node, it means you are trying to be more confident.

Let's look at the North node planets and what they represent:

The Sun:
- Popularity
- Big ego
- Karmic lessons put you in the spotlight

The Moon:
- Protective energy and the potential to have mental problems
- Popularity
- Marital success
- Success with women
- Success with your mom

Mercury:
- Clear thinking

- Good luck with your travel plans
- Great communication

Venus:
- Magnetism
- Wealth
- Self-confidence
- Beauty
- Musical talent
- Sex appeal

Mars:
- Assertive nature
- A small amount of selfishness and insensitivity toward others

Jupiter:
- Success and advancement in your career
- However, you do take success a little bit for granted

Saturn:
- Hard work will pay off
- However, you are sometimes harsh on others and yourself

Uranus:
- Fanaticism
- Sudden fame
- Creativity

Neptune:
- Artistic, psychic tendencies
- Glamorous life
- Manipulation

Pluto:
- The power to change others, the world, or even destroy them
- Healing ability
- Fame
- Obsession
- Wealth

South Node Planets

The Sun:
- Charitable
- Selflessness
- No self-confidence

The Moon:
- Quite sensitive
- Musically oriented
- Spiritually motivated

Mercury:
- Low self-esteem
- Look for comfort in sex, alcohol, drugs, or food

Mars:
- Bad temper

Jupiter:
- Informed
- Generous
- Smart
- Be careful if you play the stock market – you might lose

Saturn:
- You appreciate life's ups and downs

Uranus:
- Inspiration to others

Neptune:
- Be wary of drugs and alcohol
- Your imagination is heightened
- Trouble concentrating
- Spiritually and artistically inclined

Pluto:
- Transformative nature
- Be prepared for fame, be it for good or bad

Chapter 4: Rahu and Ketu in the Zodiac Signs

Rahu and Ketu are the lunar nodes in Vedic astrology, two important parts of an individual's birth chart. They are mathematical points, invisible if you like, indicating where the Moon and Sun intersect on their orbits. They are always opposite one another in the birth chart.

Rahu and Ketu's depiction in Vedic astrology.
Rama19920, CC BY-SA 4.0 <https://creativecommons.org/licenses/by-sa/4.0>, via Wikimedia Commons: https://commons.wikimedia.org/wiki/File:Rahu_ketu-900x900.png

Here's how they relate to the zodiac signs:

Rahu:
- **Exaltation:** Rahu is exalted in Taurus
- **Debilitation:** Rahu is debilitated in Scorpio
- **Affinity:** Rahu has no affinity for a certain sign
- **Associations:** Rahu is associated with obsession, detachment, and dissolution. No matter what sign it occupies, it amplifies its energy, creating strong attachments and desires in the areas the specific sign represents.

Ketu:
- **Exaltation:** Ketu is exalted in Scorpio
- **Debilitation:** Ketu is debilitated in Taurus
- **Affinity:** Ketu has no affinity for a certain sign
- **Associations:** Ketu is associated with spiritual growth, detachment, and dissolution. It encourages individuals to release their desires and attachments to rise above material pursuits.

Be aware that their placement in different houses also influences their effects and the aspects other planets provide them. It's also worth noting that the above effects are more nuanced and detailed when considering the placement of their house and sign in a birth chart.

Below is an easy-to-read list that shows Rahu and Ketu's positive and negative manifestations, interpretations, and the impacts of their placements in each zodiac sign. However, be aware that this is only a general overview, and things are likely to differ in individual charts:

gative manifestations, interpretations, and the impacts of their placements in each zodiac sign. However, be aware that this is only a general overview, and things are likely to differ in individual charts:

Rahu in the Zodiac Signs

Aries:
- **Interpretation:** assertiveness, ambition, drive
- **Positive Manifestation:** leadership abilities, courage, pioneering spirit
- **Negative Manifestation:** aggression, impulsiveness, selfishness

- **Placement Impact:** Influence on personal goals, self-identity, and individuality

Taurus:
- **Interpretation:** security, need for stability, materialism
- **Positive Manifestation:** resourcefulness, determination, financial expertise
- **Negative Manifestation:** stubbornness, possessiveness, greed
- **Placement Impact:** influence on possessions, wealth, and sensual desires

Gemini:
- **Interpretation:** intellectual pursuits, communications, curiosity
- **Positive Manifestation:** networking skills, adaptability, versatility
- **Negative Manifestation:** inconsistency, superficiality, restlessness
- **Placement Impact:** influence on sibling relationships, learning, communication

Cancer:
- **Interpretation:** domesticity, courage, leadership abilities
- **Positive Manifestation:** nurturing ability, empathy, intuition
- **Negative Manifestation:** clinginess, moodiness, emotional manipulation
- **Placement Impact:** influence on family dynamics, home, and emotional security

Leo:
- **Interpretation:** leadership, self-expression, creativity
- **Positive Manifestation:** charisma, confidence, artistic talent
- **Negative Manifestation:** attention-seeking, arrogance, egotism
- **Placement Impact:** influence on creativity, self-confidence, and recognition

Virgo:
- **Interpretation:** service, attention to detail, analytical thinking
- **Positive Manifestation:** problem-solving, practicality, efficiency
- **Negative Manifestation:** hypercriticism, perfectionism, anxiety
- **Placement Impact:** influence on health, work, and service-oriented activities

Libra:
- **Interpretation:** partnerships, harmony, social interactions
- **Positive Manifestation:** fairness, diplomacy, building relationships
- **Negative Manifestation:** dependency, indecisiveness, people-pleasing
- **Placement Impact:** influence on partnerships, relationships, and sense of aestheticism

Scorpio:
- **Interpretation:** transformation, intensity, depth
- **Positive Manifestation:** research abilities, perseverance, spiritual insight
- **Negative Manifestation:** obsession, manipulation, power struggles
- **Placement Impact:** influence on shared resources, intimacy, and psychological transformation

Sagittarius:
- **Interpretation:** wisdom, expansion, spiritual seeking
- **Positive Manifestation:** philosophical outlook, optimism, adventurous spirit
- **Negative Manifestation:** impulsiveness, restlessness, dogmatism
- **Placement Impact:** influence on higher education, beliefs, and travel

Capricorn:
- **Interpretation:** discipline, problem-solving, social status
- **Positive Manifestation:** leadership qualities, strategic planning, perseverance
- **Negative Manifestation:** materialistic activities, ruthlessness, workaholism
- **Placement Impact:** influence on public image, career, and long-term goals

Aquarius:
- **Interpretation:** innovation, individuality, humanitarianism
- **Positive Manifestation:** progressive thinking, originality, community involvement
- **Negative Manifestation:** eccentricity, rebellion, detachment

- **Placement Impact:** influence on friendships, social causes, and less conventional activities

Pisces:
- **Interpretation:** compassion, spirituality, imagination
- **Positive Manifestation:** artistic ability, intuition, empathy
- **Negative Manifestation:** illusion, escapism, emotionally vulnerable
- **Placement Impact:** influence on creativity, spirituality, subconscious realms

Ketu in the Zodiac Signs:

Aries:
- **Interpretation:** assertiveness, independence, initiation
- **Positive Manifestation:** the courage to break away from your limitations, self-discovery
- **Negative Manifestation:** impulsiveness, impatience, recklessness
- **Placement Impact:** influence on individuality, personal growth, and self-identity

Taurus:
- **Interpretation:** stability, sensual pleasure, material attachments
- **Positive Manifestation:** contentment with the simple things in life, detached from materialism
- **Negative Manifestation:** possessiveness, stubbornness, resisting change
- **Placement Impact:** influence on possessions, values, and a sense of security

Gemini:
- **Interpretation:** curiosity, intellect, communication
- **Positive Manifestation:** intuition in communication, detached from superficiality
- **Negative Manifestation:** scattered thinking, restlessness, challenges with communication
- **Placement Impact:** influence on expression, learning, and sibling relationships

Cancer:
- **Interpretation:** nurturing, emotionally sensitive, home
- **Positive Manifestation:** detached from emotional dependency, nurturing to bring about spiritual growth
- **Negative Manifestation:** emotional distance, overwhelming, struggling to put down roots
- **Placement Impact:** influence on family dynamics, home life, and emotional security

Leo:
- **Interpretation:** leadership, creativity, self-expression
- **Positive Manifestation:** humility, detached from ego, spiritual creativity
- **Negative Manifestation:** attention-seeking, self-centered, lack of confidence
- **Placement Impact:** influence on creative expression, self-confidence, and recognition

Virgo:
- **Interpretation:** practicality, analysis, service
- **Positive Manifestation:** spiritually serving others, detached from perfectionism
- **Negative Manifestation:** skepticism, criticalness, over-analysis
- **Placement Impact:** influence on health, work, and service-oriented activities

Libra:
- **Interpretation:** partnerships, balance, harmony
- **Positive Manifestation:** seeking balance spiritually, detached from codependency
- **Negative Manifestation:** detached from relationships, indecisiveness, struggling to find harmony
- **Placement Impact:** influence on partnerships, relationships, aesthetic sense

Scorpio:
- **Interpretation:** intensity, transformation, depth

- **Positive Manifestation:** spiritual insight, detached from power struggles
- **Negative Manifestation:** secretive behavior, obsession, fear of intimacy
- **Placement Impact:** influence on shared resources, intimacy, and psychological transformation

Sagittarius:
- **Interpretation:** wisdom, expansion, spirituality
- **Positive Manifestation:** seeking spirituality, detached from dogma, wisdom
- **Negative Manifestation:** skepticism, restlessness, spiritual escapism
- **Placement Impact:** influence on higher education, beliefs, and travel

Capricorn:
- **Interpretation:** discipline, ambition, social status
- **Positive Manifestation:** focused on inner authority, detached from worldly attachments
- **Negative Manifestation:** detached from responsibility, cynicism, fearing failure
- **Placement Impact:** influence on public image, career, and long-term goals

Aquarius:
- **Interpretation:** humanitarianism, innovation, individuality
- **Positive Manifestation:** focused on everyone's wellbeing, detached from societal norms
- **Negative Manifestation:** rebelliousness, eccentricity, detached from social connections
- **Placement Impact:** influence on friendships, social causes, non-conventional activities

Pisces:
- **Interpretation:** compassion, spirituality, imagination
- **Positive Manifestation:** spiritual insight, detached from illusions, a deep sense of empathy
- **Negative Manifestation:** confusion, escapism, no boundaries

- **Placement Impact:** influence on creativity, spirituality, and divine connection

Rahu-Ketu Axis

And to finish this chapter, the Rahu-Ketu axis interpretation in each sign and the Rahu-Ketu transit significance in the prediction of life events:

Aries-Libra Axis:
- **Rahu in Aries/Ketu in Libra:** highlights the balance between being self-assertive (Aries) and harmony in relationships (Libra.) The emphasis is on reaching the middle ground between your needs and those of others.

Taurus-Scorpio Axis:
- **Rahu in Taurus/Ketu in Scorpio:** focuses on Taurus's material stability and Scorpio's deep transformation and signifies needing to let go of material attachments and welcome inner growth,

Gemini-Sagittarius Axis:
- **Rahu in Gemini/Ketu in Sagittarius:** highlights Gemini's intellectual exploration against Sagittarius's spiritual expansion, signifying the middle ground between gaining new knowledge and looking for your higher truths.

Cancer-Capricorn Axis:
- **Rahu in Cancer/Ketu in Capricorn:** the emphasis is on Cancer's emotional nurturing against Capricorn's practical ambition, signifying professional/personal life integration and the balance of career goals and emotional wellbeing.

Leo-Aquarius Axis:
- **Rahu in Leo/Ketu in Aquarius:** emphasizes Leo's individual self-expression and Aquarius's collective ideals, signifying the middle ground between contributions to progress in society and personal creativity.

Virgo-Pisces Axis:
- **Rahu in Virgo/Ketu in Pisces:** focuses on Virgo's practical analysis and Pisces's spiritual transcendence, signifying the integration of intuition and logic and balancing spiritual connection with attention to detail.

Significance of Rahu-Ketu Transits in Predicting Life Events

The transits have a big role in this because they indicate when karmic energy shifts and areas where focus is needed. Their significance is:

- **Karmic Lessons and Life Direction**: The transits uncover karmic lessons and areas in life where attention is needed, along with growth. They also indicate when focus shifts and help individuals align with their direction and life purpose.
- **Major Transformations**: the transits tend to coincide with internal and external life events, usually major ones. They can bring breakthroughs in something you've struggled with, sudden change, and can even change your perception, all leading to improved personal growth.
- **Triggers Past-Life Karma:** Rahu-Ketu transits can awaken past-life karma, never resolved issues coming back to the forefront. These transits allow you to heal, let go of your karmic baggage and release old, repetitive patterns.
- **Challenges and Opportunities**: the transits provide individuals with a mix of challenges and opportunities. Rahu influences new possibilities and desires, while Ketu influences spiritual growth and quick detachment.
- **Event Timing**: these transits may coincide with something significant happening in your life, such as changes in a relationship, a new job or promotion in your existing one, a major decision, or a spiritual awakening. Further insights can be gained from the placement of the aspects and houses during the transit.

Now let's move on to Rahu and Ketu in the twelve houses.

Chapter 5: Rahu and Ketu in the Twelve Houses

The twelve zodiac houses are just one small part of the birth chart puzzle, but they offer up quite a bit of interesting information. For example, do you know the difference between the sun being the first house at your time of birth or the twelfth house? Understanding these things can help you determine why you are outgoing when your partner or best friend is quieter and more reserved. Or understanding the sign ruling the tenth house can give you some idea of how to achieve your professional goals.

Let's take the time to learn the basics of the twelve houses and what information they can provide about you and your life path.

The Twelve Houses Defined

Think of your birth chart as a snapshot, showing the sky as it was at the time of your birth. The houses indicate where the planets, including the Sun and Moon, were positioned when and where you were born.

Sample depiction of the Bhavas in Vedic astrology.
Rajeshodayanchal, CC BY-SA 3.0 <https://creativecommons.org/licenses/by-sa/3.0>, via Wikimedia Commons: https://commons.wikimedia.org/wiki/File:Bhava-chakra.svg

The houses represent how the Earth rotates on its axis every 24 hours. As the Earth rotates, the planets and sun appear to move clockwise through the houses. They rise on the first house's cusp in the east – the left of the chart. At midday, it hovers at the top of the chart and then moves to the west, on the right side of the chart, to set. Around midnight, it hovers at the bottom of the chart.

Think of it as a star map drawn up just for you. However, it is much more than this. The location of the Sun, Moon, and the colors of the planets indicate expressions as they each represent a part of your life. This will be discussed more in a while.

What Do the Houses Mean?

The houses are often called zones or sectors on your birth chart. However, each has a self-explanatory name representing a different aspect of your life and existence. Understanding each house's meaning can help you better understand your overall life, so here's a brief overview of each house, its name, and its meaning.

The First House

Alternative Names: House of Self, House of Appearance, House of Identity

Sanskrit Name: Lagna Bhava

Meaning:

The first house is the Rising Sign or the Ascendant, and, as the name indicates, it represents your physical appearance, self-image, personality, and how you let the world see you. It is associated with your sense of self and approach.

The Second House

Alternative Names: House of Possessions, House of Values, House of Finances

Sanskrit Name: Dhana Bhava

Meaning:

The second house relates to your finances, material possessions, self-worth, and personal resources. It is associated with your financial values and attitude toward possessions and money.

The Third House

Alternative Names: House of Communication, House of Learning, House of Siblings

Sanskrit Name: Sahaja Bhava

Meaning:

This house is about communication, intellect, language, and learning, but it also governs relationships with your siblings, immediate environment, and neighbors. The third house also represents mental activities, writing, and short journeys.

The Fourth House

Alternative Names: House of Home, House of Roots, House of Family

Sanskrit Name: Sukha Bhava

Meaning:

The fourth house represents family, home, emotional security, and ancestry. It relates to your inner experiences, private life, and the true foundation of who you are. It is associated with a sense of belonging and your relationships with your mother and father.

The Fifth House

Alternative Names: House of Creativity, house of Children, House of Pleasure

Sanskrit Name: Putra Bhava

Meaning:

This house represents artistic activities, love affairs, hobbies, and your relationship with children. It is associated with romance, entertainment, pleasure, creativity, and self-expression.

The Sixth House

Alternative Names: House of Service, House of Work, House of Health

Sanskrit Name: Shatru Bhava

Meaning:

The sixth house is connected to health, daily routines, service, and work, and it governs how you approach your responsibilities, work environment, and physical wellbeing. It is associated with organization, habits, and service to others.

The Seventh House

Alternative Names: House of Partnerships, House of Others, House of Marriage

Sanskrit Name: Kalatra Bhava

Meaning:

The seventh house is about partnerships, relationships, cooperation, and marriage. It represents how you interact with others, such as business partners and colleagues, personal relationships, and enemies.

The Eighth House

Alternative Names: House of Transformation, House of Rebirth, House of Sex

Sanskrit Name: Randhra Bhava

Meaning:

The eighth house concerns sexuality, transformation, emotional bonds, and shared resources. It relates to big changes in your life, the concepts of death and being reborn, and represents intimacy, inheritance, matters of the occult, and psychological growth.

The Ninth House
Alternative Names: House of Expansion, House of Higher Learning, House of Philosophy

Sanskrit Name: Bhagya Bhava

Meaning:
The ninth house represents philosophy, higher knowledge, beliefs, long-distance travel, and spirituality. It's about religion, higher knowledge, law, and cultural experiences and is about your connection with the wider world and search for meaning.

The Tenth House
Alternative Names: House of Career, House of Public Life, House of Status

Sanskrit Name: Karma Bhava

Meaning:
This house concerns public image, career, social status, and reputation. It represents achievement, ambition, and how you relate to authority figures and is associated with how the public sees you and your professional goals.

The Eleventh House
Alternative Names: House of Hopes and Dreams, House of Community, House of Friends

Sanskrit Name: Labha Bhava

Meaning:
The eleventh house represents your goals, aspirations, friendships, and social groups. It relates to group activities, community groups, and humanitarian causes you are involved in and reflects those who support you and your ideals.

The Twelfth House
Alternative Names: House of Spirituality, House of the Unconscious, House of Karma

Sanskrit Name: Vyaya Bhava

Meaning:
The final house is connected to the unconscious mind, spirituality, hidden matters, and solitude. It represents karma, self-reflection,

transcendence, and healing and is associated with retreat, meditation, dreams, and your psyche's subconscious aspects.

Rahu and Ketu in Each House

Lastly, we'll look at Rahu and Ketu in each house, including their interpretations and characteristics, good and bad traits, and the impact of their placement.

First House
Rahu

Interpretation:
- Ambition
- A need for recognition
- Unconventional identity

Positive Traits:
- Leadership
- Courage
- A unique personal style

Negative Traits:
- Egotistic
- Self-centered
- Restless

Placement Impact:

Influences physical appearance, self-image, and personal goals

Ketu

Interpretation:
- Spiritual growth
- Detachment
- Selflessness

Positive Traits:
- Intuitive insight
- Humility
- Non-attachment

Negative Traits:
- Self-doubt
- Insecurity
- Empty feelings

Placement Impact:
Influences spiritual pursuits, self-awareness, self-identity

Second House
Rahu
Interpretation:
- Financial growth
- Materialistic desires
- Unconventional values

Positive Traits:
- Ambition
- Financial Expertise
- Resourcefulness

Negative Traits:
- Obsessed with material possessions
- Greed
- Financial instability

Placement Impact:
Influences personal values, accumulating wealth, and speech

Ketu
Interpretation:
- Spiritual values
- Detached from material possessions
- Unconventional talent

Positive Traits:
- Inner wisdom
- Not attached to material wealth
- Self-sufficient

Negative Traits:
- Struggles to express self-worth
- Financial challenges
- Detached from material stability

Placement Impact:
Influences finances, self-worth, and values

Third House
Rahu
Interpretation:
- Curiosity
- Communication skills
- Desire to learn and network

Positive Traits:
- Adaptability
- Versatility
- Networking ability

Negative Traits:
- Restlessness
- Gossip
- Inconsistency

Placement Impact:
Influences learning, communication, and sibling relationships

Ketu
Interpretation:
- Detached from superficial communication
- Spiritual activities
- Intuitive insight

Positive Traits:
- Depth of thought
- Intuition
- Spiritual exploration

Negative Traits:
- Social detachment
- Communication challenges
- Struggling with short-term endeavors

Placement Impact:
Influences sibling relationships, learning style, and intuition

Fourth House

Rahu

Interpretation:
- Family ambition
- Need for emotional security
- Non-conventional home life

Positive Traits:
- Domestic affair ambitions
- Ability to nurture
- Growth-oriented family life

Negative Traits:
- Emotional manipulation
- Overly attached to home
- Disrupted family life

Placement Impact:
Influences family dynamics, home environment, and emotional security

Ketu

Interpretation:
- Detached from emotional attachments
- Introspection leading to spiritual growth

Positive Traits:
- Intuitive insight
- Emotionally independent
- Deeply self-understanding

Negative Traits:
- Emotionally distanced
- Struggles to establish roots
- Unsettled in the home

Placement Impact:

Influences ancestral heritage connection, inner peace, and emotional wellbeing

Fifth House

Rahu

Interpretation:
- Need for recognition
- A progressive approach to romance
- Creative activities

Positive Traits:
- Creativity
- Leadership qualities
- Ambitious in artistic activities

Negative Traits:
- Arrogant
- Attention seeker
- Behavior in speculation and love is risky

Placement Impact:

Influences creativity, individuality expression, and romance

Ketu

Interpretation:
- Spiritual insights
- Detached from the egoic desire
- Non-conventional parenting approach

Positive Traits:
- Detached from outcomes
- Inner wisdom
- Unique approach to self-expression

Negative Traits:
- Lack of confidence in creative activities
- Self-doubt
- Challenges in romantic partnerships

Placement Impact:
Influences creativity, self-expression, and experiences with kids

Sixth House
Rahu
Interpretation:
- Desires success in service and work
- Non-conventional methods of healing

Positive Traits:
- Determination
- Novel approach to healing
- Problem-solving skills
- Work efficiency

Negative Traits:
- Workaholic
- Conflict in roles related to service

Placement Impact:
Influences health, work environment, and service to others

Ketu
Interpretation:
- Detached from routine jobs
- Selfless service leading to spiritual growth

Positive Traits:
- Selflessness
- Compassion
- Abilities in holistic healing

Negative Traits:
- Avoids responsibility
- Indecisiveness

- Health challenges

Placement Impact:
Influences daily routine, health, and activities related to service

Seventh House

Rahu

Interpretation:
- Non-conventional relationships
- Desire for partnerships
- Ambitious collaborations

Positive Traits:
- Business expertise
- Diplomacy
- Growth-oriented partnerships

Negative Traits:
- Codependency
- Unpredictability in relationships
- Manipulative

Placement Impact:
Influences marriage, partnerships, and public interaction

Ketu

Interpretation:
- Not attached to dependent relationships
- Solitude leading to spiritual growth

Positive Traits:
- Spiritual insight
- Independence
- Self-reliance

Negative Traits:
- Detached from relationships
- Struggles to form relationships
- Uncompromising

Placement Impact:

Influences marriage, partnerships, and the balance between shared and personal interests

Eighth House

Rahu

Interpretation:
- Need for transformation
- Interests in the occult
- Non-conventional way of approaching shared assets

Positive Traits:
- Investigative abilities
- Intensity
- Power to transform

Negative Traits:
- Manipulative
- Obsessed with control
- Emotional and financial instability

Placement Impact:

Influences inheritance, shared resources, and psychological transformation

Ketu

Interpretation:
- Detached from attachments
- Releasing the ego, leading to spiritual growth

Positive Traits:
- Insight into the mysteries of life and death
- Ability to surrender
- Inner transformation

Negative Traits:
- Fears intimacy
- Struggles to manage shared resources
- Faces challenges in rebirth and healing

Placement Impact:
Influences shared resources, transformation, and interests in the occult

Ninth House

Rahu

Interpretation:
- Wants expansion
- Ambitious in higher knowledge
- Non-conventional beliefs

Positive Traits:
- Adventurous
- Growth-related activities
- Philosophical insight

Negative Traits:
- Restless
- Dogmatic
- No regard for the cultural norms

Placement Impact:
Influences spirituality, higher education, and long-distance journeys

Ketu

Interpretation:
- Detached from dogma, intuitive wisdom – leading to spiritual growth

Positive Traits:
- Detached from beliefs
- Intuition
- Profound spiritual experiences

Negative Traits:
- No faith
- Skeptical
- Challenges in long-distance journeys and higher education

Placement Impact:
Influences higher education, spiritual beliefs, and exploring new horizons

Tenth House
Rahu
Interpretation:
- Need for public recognition
- Career ambitions
- Non-conventional authority

Positive Traits:
- Ambition
- Original approach to career
- Leadership qualities

Negative Traits:
- Manipulative for personal gain
- Career instability
- Doesn't hold traditional hierarchies in high regard

Placement Impact:
Influences public image, career, and achievements

Ketu
Interpretation:
- Detached from worldly success
- An inner calling to service
- Service to others leading to spiritual growth

Positive Traits:
- Detached from societal expectations
- Humility
- Inner calling to service

Negative Traits:
- Unambitious
- Struggles with authority
- Career advancement challenges

Placement Impact:
Influences public image, vocational calling, and a sense of purpose

Eleventh House
Rahu
Interpretation:
- Need for social connections
- Community involvement ambitions
- Non-conventional friendships

Positive Traits:
- Philanthropic efforts
- Networking abilities
- Friendships related to personal growth

Negative Traits:
- Opportunist
- Detached from real connections
- Socially manipulative

Placement Impact:
Influences aspirations, social circles, and community involvement

Ketu
Interpretation:
- Detached from social connections
- Inner fulfillment leading to spiritual growth

Positive Traits:
- Detached from the expectations of society
- Intuitive in gaining insight into collective needs
- Spiritual friendships

Negative Traits:
- Struggles to form long-term friendships
- Socially detached
- Feels out of place in group settings

Placement Impact:
Influences aspirations, social networks, and connections to similar people

Twelfth House
Rahu
Interpretation:
- Need to grow spiritually
- Escapism
- Non-conventional interests

Positive Traits:
- Empathetic
- Can navigate through unseen realms
- Mystical activities

Negative Traits:
- Delusional
- Isolated from reality
- addicted

Placement Impact:

Influences the unconscious mind, spirituality, and retreating from materialism

Ketu
Interpretation:
- Detached from worldly desires
- Introspection and surrender leading to spiritual growth

Positive Traits:
- Enlightened
- Not attached to illusions
- Hidden knowledge insights

Negative Traits:
- Lonely
- Escapism
- Struggles with boundaries

Placement Impact:

Influences the subconscious mind, spirituality, and detachment from materialism

It's time to turn our attention to Karma and Karmic lessons.

Chapter 6: Karmic Lessons

Karmic astrology also goes by the name of soul-centered or evolutionary astrology. It is an astrological branch focused on Karma and the evolutionary journey your soul takes, digging into the idea that you carry with you parts of your past lives, lessons, and experiences that may go some way toward shaping your present life.

Karmic astrology treats an individual's birth chart as a map showing their soul's evolutionary path. The birth chart looks at the planet's aspects and placement and the North and South nodes, which are believed to represent an individual's evolutionary intentions and karmic lessons.

One of the principles of Karmic astrology is personal growth and free will.
https://unsplash.com/photos/r2nJPbEYuSQ?utm_source=unsplash&utm_medium=referral&utm_content=creditShareLink

Key Principles

Some of the key principles of Karmic Astrology are:

- **Reincarnation and Karma:** Karmic astrologers strongly believe in reincarnation. They believe the soul lives through several lives, learning and evolving from each one. The suggestion is that what you do in past lives leaves an imprint on you, influencing what you experience in your present life.
- **Lunar Nodes:** Rahu and Ketu, the North and South nodes, respectively, are important in Vedic astrology, even more so in Karmic astrology. They represent the evolutionary journey the soul takes. Rahu indicates where you should be heading, while Ketu represents the patterns and tendencies from your past lives.
- **Karmic Lessons and Life Purpose:** Karmic astrology looks at where the lunar nodes are placed and, to help determine life purpose and karmic lessons, it also examines their aspects concerning other planets. The North node indicates where development and growth are needed in an individual's life, while the South node represents things you brought with you from your past lives.
- **Soul Contracts and Relationships:** This astrology looks into the idea that a soul enters a contract or agreement with another soul before incarnation. This results in relationships forming to ensure learning and growth. Karmic astrology studies birth charts and the dynamics to understand Karmic lessons and connections.
- **Healing and Integration:** It provides insights into an individual's challenges, wounds, and karmic patterns. Understanding and recognizing these patterns allows you to work toward integration and healing and evolve spiritually.
- **Personal Growth and Free Will:** Karmic astrology may focus on what you bring from your past lives, but it also highlights that you have free will and must take personal responsibility for your life. Everyone can work consciously with their karmic lessons and make the right choices, leading to positive transformation and personal growth.

Karmic astrology gives everyone a framework to help them understand their life journey and its spiritual dimensions. It provides self-reflection, guidance, and a deep insight into the soul's evolutionary journey, and it helps you work through karmic challenges and align with your life purpose.

Karmic Astrology and Its Role in Vedic Astrology

Karmic astrology has an important role to play in Vedic astrology because it aligns with Hinduism principles, spiritual and philosophical. Hinduism is an ancient Indian tradition and is where Vedic astrology originated. Here's why karmic astrology is important in Vedic astrology:

- **Understanding the Law of Cause and Effect:** Vedic astrology acknowledges this law which tells you that, for every action, there are consequences, and these can reach far into your present life. Karmic astrology helps you understand what's happening in your life now, the challenges you face, and the opportunities that come your way are all directly related to things you did in past lives. It encourages you to take responsibility for your actions and empowers you to shape your life by making conscious choices.

- **Exploring the Soul's Journey:** Vedic astrology strongly believes in reincarnation, where an individual's soul is incarnated several times, each time learning and evolving. Karmic astrology helps you to dig into your soul's journey, showing you unresolved issues, karmic debt, and lessons from past lives that influence your present life. When you can understand the patterns, you can start working on balancing your Karma and resolving issues to help you grow spiritually.

- **Identifying Our Purpose in Life:** Karmic astrology helps you identify your purpose in life – or your *dharma*. It tells you about your strengths, talents, and challenges, which are usually related to experiences from your past lives. When you understand the karmic lessons and your potential, you can ensure your actions align with your life purpose, which leads to better personal growth and inner fulfillment.

- **Guides Us in Transformation and Healing:** Karmic astrology is a tool that helps you to self-reflect and aids in transformation. It helps you identify and recognize limitations, patterns, and unresolved issues getting in the way of progress. A deep understanding of these challenges' karmic roots can help you

work consciously toward transformation and healing, thus improving circumstances in your present life and for the future.
- **Predictive Insights:** Karmic astrology uses past Karma to let you see the possibilities and our potential for the future. It lets astrologers identify the Karmic patterns and understand how they influence future life. When you can recognize the challenges and opportunities that come your way, you can be more aware as you work through life's choices and ensure your decisions align with your purpose in life.

Karmic astrology is important in Vedic astrology, providing a holistic view of your life journeys. It emphasizes the importance and significance of spiritual growth, personal responsibility, and making conscious choices in life.

Different Types of Karma

Vedic astrology acknowledges several types of Karma based on an individual's intentions and actions. The different types are reflective of the consequences of past actions and how they influence our present and future life and experiences.

These are the most common types of Vedic Karma:
- **Sanchita Karma** refers to Karma that an individual has accumulated from past lives and taken into their present life. It represents all their negative and positive actions, including those not yet experienced or resolved. Sanchita Karma influences the opportunities and circumstances an individual faces in their present life.
- **Prarabdha Karma** is a subset of Sanchita, referring to the ripe section of accumulated Karma, the section an individual is meant to experience in their current life. It represents situations, experiences, and challenges an individual is predestined to face during their present life. Prarabdha Karma is considered the destiny a person faces and has to work through.
- **Kriyamana Karma:** also called Agami Karma, this Karma is created by an individual's current choices and actions. It includes all the intentions, actions, and decisions a person makes in their current life, contributing to their future experiences. Kriyamana Karma may intensify or mitigate the effects of Sanchita Karma's

accumulations.

- **Anarabdha Karma refers to Karma that hasn't started manifesting yet, latent or dormant Karma, or the Karmic seeds that** have been planted but haven't begun to grow. These potentials can stay hidden until the time is right for their activation.

One important thing to note is that all these types of Karma are not actually considered separate, as they are all aspects of Karma dynamics. They are all connected, influence one another, and play a part in shaping a person's spiritual growth and life experiences.

Karmic Debt

Karmic debt and the philosophy of Karma are connected. Karmic debt is all about an individual's actions in their previous lives working to influence their present life's quality and nature. What you did and how you acted in past lives can push your energy out of balance, creating a "debt" that you face as limitations, challenges, or tough situations in your current life.

Vedic astrology tells you that everyone was born with their own astrological birth chart, showing where all the celestial bodies were at the exact time and place of their birth. This chart tells you of your past lives and Karmic influences, and certain aspects, positions, and combinations of planets are said to highlight Karmic debts that you need to resolve in your present life.

Karmic debt is usually associated with where Rahu and Ketu are positioned in an individual's birth chart. Rahu is all about material goals, attachments, and desires, while Ketu is about detachment, spiritual growth, and Karmic lessons. The specific houses in which the two lunar nodes are placed and their aspects to different planets can all indicate where an individual needs to take care of things.

Just because a birth chart shows Karmic debt, it doesn't mean it is negative. It tells you there are areas of learning, growth, and evolution that you need to take advantage of. When you can recognize your Karmic debts, you can learn to be self-reflective, make conscious choices, and do whatever is necessary to resolve your Karmic imbalances.

Signs of Karmic Debt
1. You Can't Explain Some Patterns and Behaviors

Suppose you experience certain patterns or behaviors or an irrational fear of something that doesn't make sense to you in your present life. In that case, there's a good chance it heralds from one of your past lives.

Be it a hatred of all things happy, distrust in authority, or a fear of water, anything your present life can't explain is likely a result of Karmic debt.

2. Mastery Opportunities

If you do nothing to settle it, Karmic debt will continue to make itself known, coercing you to settle the score and master Karma. Incomplete Karmic cycles are much like any pattern; if you don't build up your self-awareness, they will become a habit. Keep ignoring it, and your incomplete Karma will just pile up.

3. You've Had Karmic Relationships

Sometimes, Karmic debt is related to relationships you may have had in your past lives. Karmic relationships are intense. Some people unknowingly seek consistently turbulent relationships, which could result from something that happened in a past life. While these relationships are likely toxic, you must experience this type of relationship if you can pay your Karmic debt off.

4. You Know of at Least One Repetitive Theme in Your Life

Whether you try to ignore your Karmic debts or not, it's a fair bet you know the themes that repeat themselves throughout your life. Incomplete Karma can make you feel like you are trapped, and you can't brush this aside. This kind of debt can be overwhelming, but even though it's tough to overcome, you have to do it.

5. You Have One or More Karmic Debt Numbers

If you do a personal numerology chart, you may discover you have Karmic debt numbers. They will be one of the following:

- 13
- 14
- 16
- 19

Let's see what they are.

Karmic Debt Numbers

You will be shown how to calculate your numbers in a bit, but first, here's a look at them:

- **13:** if you have a Karmic debt number of 13, it means you were selfish and lazy in your previous life. When things go wrong, you tend to blame everyone but yourself, and you won't take responsibility for anything. You are typically negative and may also be stubborn and quite controlling. In this case, your Karma dictates that you are accountable for your actions.

- **14:** the number 14 indicates that you abuse freedom through serious self-indulgence or domination of others. You will likely over-indulge, struggle with self-control, and you will find commitment hard. In this case, your Karma is to be self-disciplined and vulnerable in terms of other people.
- **16:** an incredibly challenging debt number, and you may struggle to overcome it. This could be because you had a very strong ego in a past life and struggled in relationships with other people. You may have experienced a fair number of relationships that didn't work out, struggled to connect with others, and were an egotist. Your Karma is to consider how your actions affect others and be more considerate of them.
- **19:** a Karmic debt number of 19 says that you are completely independent and self-reliant and may have treated others poorly in one or more of your past lives. You may be narcissistic, selfish, and/or manipulative, your public image is more important to you than anything, and you see personal success where there is none. Your Karma is prioritizing others, caring for them, and considering their feelings.

Figuring Out Your Debt

Although this book is primarily concerned with Vedic astrology and the lunar nodes, it would be remiss not to tell you how to determine your Karmic debt in numerology. It's not hard to do; your birth chart has five core numbers on it, each influencing you as a person and your purpose in life. Find those numbers on your chart and look at how they were calculated; the number will indicate if you need to repay a debt.

Here's how to work the numbers out:

Personality:

Self-explanatory, this tells you what personality type you are and how your relationships play out. Working it out is simple; take the month and date of your birthday and add all the digits together. Let's say it is 4th September; add 0 + 4 + 9, and you get 13.

Relationship to Debt:

To reduce 13 to a single number, add 1 +3, which equals 4. That is your personality number, but because the 1 and 3 are 13, that's your Karmic debt number.

Life Path:

Your life path number is similar to your sun sign in Vedic astrology and is calculated by adding your birth date numbers, as above, but with the year added in.

Relationship to Debt:

With a birth date of 14th August 2001, you add them like this: 1 + 4 + 8 + 2 + 0 + 0 + 1, which equals 16. 1 + 6 equals 7 (your life path number), and 16 is your Karmic debt number.

Expression:

This is about your passions and abilities, and you find the number by adding your name digits together using the following chart:

1: A, J, S
2: B, K, T
3: C, L, U
4: D, M, V
5: E, N, W
6: F, O, X
7: G, P, Y
8: H, Q, Z
9: I, R

Relationship to Debt:

Let's assume your name is Jackson. Using the chart above, you would add 1 + 1 + 3 + 2 + 1 + 6 + 5, which equals 19. Your Expression number is 1 + 9, which equals 10 reduced to 1 + 0 = 1, and your Karmic debt number is 19.

Birthdate:

This is just the date you were born, indicating skills you carry with you from your past lives.

Relationship to Debt:

If your birth date is the 13th, your birthdate number is 1 + 3 = 4, but your Karmic debt is 13.

Soul Urge:

This is the last core number and relates to your heart's desires. Work out the numbers for each consonant in your name – first, middle, and last – and add them together. Only the consonants count here, not the vowels.

Relationship to Debt:

Let's use the example of a person called Jane Doe. Add the numbers for the consonants: J + N + D, which is 1 + 5 + 4, which equals 10. Now add 1 + 0 to bring this down to 1, your soul urge number, and you have a Karmic debt number of 10. This tells you you don't have a Karmic debt because 10 represents a complete Karma.

Karmic Planetary Positions and Karmic Houses

The Karmic Houses and the Karmic planetary positions play a considerable role in helping you understand your own Karmic patterns and the lessons you must learn in your present lifetime. Here's a breakdown of them:

Karmic Planetary Positions:

This refers to where certain planets are placed in a birth chart and their condition. These planets are thought to have implications for an individual's Karma. The important planets are:

- Saturn
- Rahu – North Node
- Ketu – South Node Let's look at these individually:

1. **Saturn:** The most signific planet in terms of Karma, it tells us where challenges may lie in a person's life, where they might struggle in the future or face tough responsibilities. Its placement in the birth chart and its aspects to other planets indicate where an individual might face growth opportunities and Karmic tests. Saturn's influence can provide several lessons that lead to spiritual and personal development, including perseverance, discipline, and maturity.

2. **Rahu and Ketu:** these are the lunar nodes, and, in Vedic astrology, they are considered to characterize the Karmic axis. Rahu is about

future growth, ambition, and desire, while Ketu is about detachment, spiritual evolution, and past-life experiences. Their positions in your birth chart tell you what Karmic areas need attention in your current life. Rahu's influence provides opportunities to use worldly experiences for personal growth, while Ketu's provides the encouragement to detach from material things and develop spiritually.

Karmic Houses

The Karmic Houses are houses associated with Karmic lessons and themes. They are:
- First House
- Fourth House
- Eight House
- Ninth House
- Twelfth House
- Tenth House – occasionally Here's a breakdown:

1. **The First House** is the house of self, also representing your life path and personality. Significant aspects or planets in the first house indicate Karmic lessons and patterns related to personal growth, self-expression, and self-identity.
2. **The Fourth House** is the house of home and represents family and emotional foundations. When Karmic influences arise in this house, they typically represent unresolved issues or challenges that arise due to emotional wellbeing, ancestral patterns, and family dynamics.
3. **The Eighth House** is the house of transformation, also representing aspects of your life you keep hidden and secrets. Karmic influences usually revolve around lessons related to sexuality, shared resources, deep psychological patterns, and power dynamics.
4. **The Ninth House** is the house of higher education, also representing beliefs and spirituality. Karmic influences include lessons about spiritual growth, philosophical beliefs, and your search for truth and meaning.
5. **The Twelfth House** is the house of spirituality, also representing hidden realms and the subconscious mind. When Karmic

influences arise in this house, they usually relate to solitude, releasing Karmic attachments, spiritual growth, and past-life memories.

6. **The Tenth House** occasionally appears in a birth chart and is the house of career, public image, and social status. When karmic influences arise, they usually revolve around lessons on integrity, your life purpose, and Karmic responsibilities in public.

Of course, these are just some factors involved in analyzing Karmic Houses and planetary positions. The birth chart should include conjunctions, aspects, and other influences to completely understand Karmic lessons and patterns.

It's time to put all you've learned into practice as this guide moves on to birth charts.

Chapter 7: Birth Chart Samples

In Vedic astrology, a birth chart is known as a natal chart, horoscope, or Janam Kundli. This diagram indicates the position of the planets when you were born, akin to being a plan of your life if you like. It tells you about your personality, what you are like as a person, and about your strengths and weaknesses. It is also about your potential in life and what events you may have to face down the line.

Key Elements

These are the key elements of a Kundli according to Vedic astrology:

1. **The Planets:** a Kundli shows where the nine primary planets, as per Vedic astrology, are placed. Those planets are known as the Navagrahas, and they are:
   - Sun
   - Moon
   - Mars
   - Mercury
   - Jupiter
   - Venus
   - Saturn
   - Rahu – the North Node
   - Ketu – the South Node

Each planet represents a specific life aspect with its own implications and qualities.

2. **The Signs** are the Zodiac signs, also called Rashis, based on Sidereal astrology. Each sign represents certain characteristics and traits which influence the specific planets in them.
3. **The Houses:** a Kundli is separated into 12 houses or Bhavas. Each represents a specific aspect of life, like career, family, wealth, spirituality, etc. Where planets are placed in these houses indicates the aspect of life where they express energy.
4. **The Ascendant:** the sign that rose in the East at the time of your birth, also called Lagna. It is considered the most important part of a birth chart because it represents the person's demeanor, physical appearance, and how they approach life. This sets the tone for the whole chart.
5. **Aspects:** in Vedic astrology, aspects are the relationships between each planet. The aspects are how each planet influences the houses or other planets, thus influencing certain areas of an individual's life and creating the dynamics between the energies from the different planets.
6. **Divisional Charts:** in Vedic astrology, divisional charts are used to give more detail on certain areas of life. These charts, also called Vargas, each focus on certain aspects of life.

Different Types of Birth Charts

There are different types of birth charts, which are the most common.

The South Indian Chart

This chart depicts the zodiac in its exact layout. However, rather than the circle typically used in Western astrology, it uses a square with twelve smaller boxes. Each box represents a Rashi or zodiac sign and is always located in the same boxes. Look at the diagram below; the empty box in the middle is planet Earth, and the rest are the zodiac belt, a surrounding "circle" of the zodiac signs:

PISCES	ARIES	TAURUS	GEMINI
AQUARIUS			CANCER
CAPRICORN			LEO
SAGITTARIUS	SCORPIO	LIBRA	VIRGO

This is a Rashi-based chart. When the chart has been completed, it will show the planets in the box with the zodiac sign the planet is placed in. The Ascendant or Rising Sign will be shown in the right box, denoted by one of two things:
- A diagonal line across the box
- Marking the box with Lagna or ASC

Advantages:

The biggest advantage is that South Indian birth charts are incredibly accurate in predicting life events and make it easy to understand how the planets influence an individual. They are also detailed, offering a complex analysis of the different aspects of an individual's life and showing planetary aspects and positions. Because this chart has deep connections with ancient Indian spirituality, allowing us to see how the individual and the cosmos are connected. This gives an accurate insight into Karmic patterns and purpose in life. You can move the Ascendant or choose another planetary aspect for a different view on this chart; you don't need to draw up a new one.

That said, if you've been looking at the aspects on other charts, this one will require you to do a little counting, but, like anything, practice makes perfect. Counting is simple; go to the top row and find Aries – tip: it will always be in the same box, top center. Then count in a clockwise direction. Numbers are not required in any box because the signs have fixed positions on this chart. Finding the house numbers is also simple; just start counting from the Lagna. You can always put the houses on the chart if it makes it easier for you.

You can compare a Rashi and South Indian chart very easily; just put them side-by-side. Because the Rashis don't move, you can easily see where an individual's planet is relative to another individual's planet. For example, you could find both partners' Moons in a relationship reading and determine whether the relationship will work.

Because each Rashi is allocated to the same box, populating it with planets is much easier, not having to squeeze them into oddly shaped, smaller sections.

The North Indian Chart

Often known as a diamond format, this chart is more astrological and less astronomical. Where the South Indian chart is based on Rashis, this one is based more on the Houses and the Rashis change boxes. The top box in the chart will always be the first, and the lowest is always the seventh.

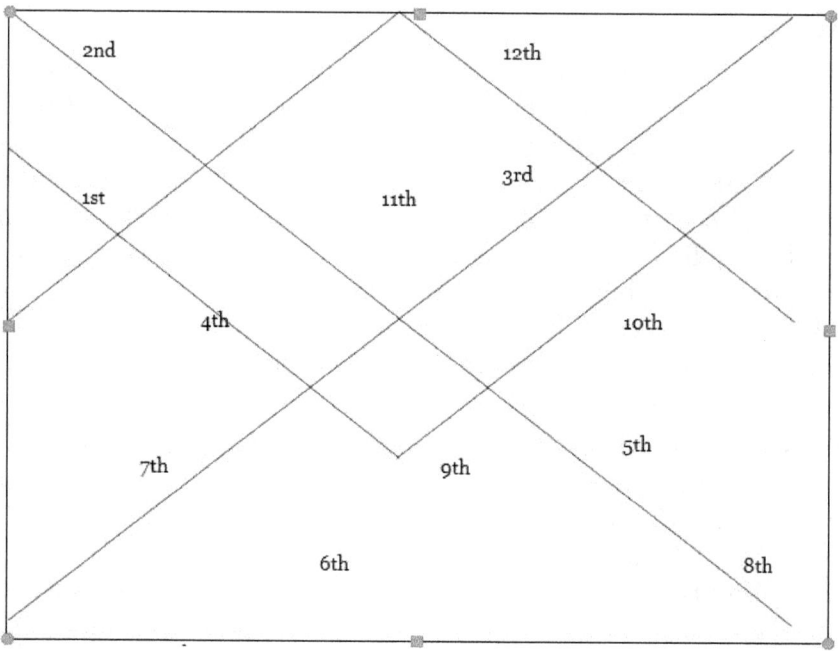

Advantages:

The first house is always in the top diamond in the middle, and counting starts from this and moves anticlockwise. The biggest advantage is that the house in which a planet is allocated can be seen at a glance. However, the entire chart must be drawn again if a Moon or Chandra Lagna chart is required.

Without numbering, the North Indian chart is not very useful; each house's Rashi can only be determined with numbers. In this chart, the numbers indicate the Rashis, and they are numbered as follows:

- 1 – Aries (Mesha)
- 2 – Taurus (Varisabha)
- 3 – Gemini (Mithuna)
- 4 – Cancer (Karka)
- 5 – Leo (Simha)
- 6 – Virgo (Kanya)
- 7 – Libra (Tula)
- 8 – Scorpio (Vrischika)
- 9 – Sagittarius (Dhanusas)
- 10 – Capricorn (Makara)
- 11 – Aquarius (Kumbha)
- 12 – Pisces (Meena)

This chart makes a synastry comparison by house simple, but a Rashi comparison is not so easy, especially for newbies.

The East Indian Chart

A kind of blend between the last two charts, the East Indian chart is based on the Rashis, and Aries is always fixed in the same position – top middle box. Counting is anticlockwise, house counting is done manually, and the Lagna will always be shown in the correct box.

TAURUS GEMINI	ARIES	PISCES AQUARIUS
CANCER		CAPRICORN
LEO VIRGO	LIBRA	SAGITTARIUS SCORPIO

Advantages:

The East Indian and South Indian charts have the same advantages. It closely matches the astronomical layout, with the Earth in the center and the zodiac belt around it, and it is easier to see the planets' dignities. However, newbies may find it difficult to count houses as they must manually count from the Ascendant.

It's also to see the chart from different aspects without needing to draw it again. Because the Rashis always stay in the same place, numbering is not required.

The Western Zodiac Wheel

Western astrology uses a wheel diagram for the birth chart, giving us a literal look at the Earth surrounded by the Rashis. The zodiacs encompass 360 degrees, which are shown in the chart as 12 equal divisions. The Ascendant is always shown on the left, and the Rashis go anticlockwise.

This chart shows the placement of the planters - precisely to the degree - making it simple to see how the planets interplay with one another.

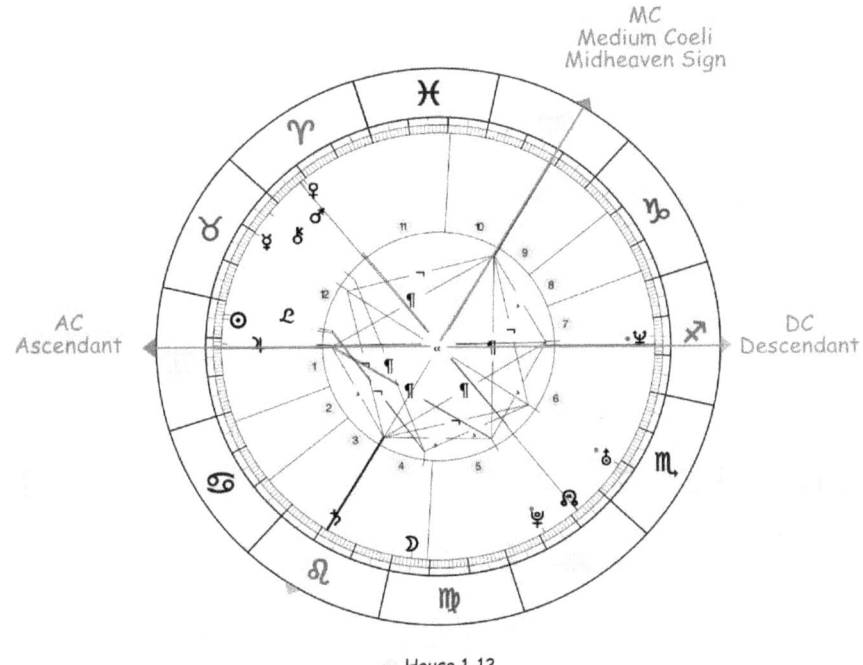

House 1-12
Western zodiac wheel sample.
Chrish73, CC BY-SA 4.0 <https://creativecommons.org/licenses/by-sa/4.0>, via Wikimedia Commons: https://commons.wikimedia.org/wiki/File:Horoscope_-_where_to_find_ascendant_descendant_and_midheaven_sign.jpg

Advantages

The advantages of using the Western Zodiac wheel are that it is simple, widely recognized, and easier for many people to understand. It also uses a psychological approach, with more focus on an individual's personality, strengths, challenges, and motivations. As an astrology chart, it is continually evolving, especially as new planets are being discovered, and it also makes it easy to compare two individuals in terms of compatibility. To compare charts, you need two circles; the outer circle shows the information for one chart, while the inner circle shows information for the other.

Now to the interesting part – decoding your birth chart. The next chapter is quite long and involved, so be sure you understand everything you have read up until now. When you are ready, let's get decoding.

Chapter 8: Decoding Your Birth Chart

A kundli is a birth chart, a diagram used to evaluate and predict an individual's future. To create one, an astrologer will require some details from you, including your exact time, date, and place of birth. Vedic astrologers use birth charts or Kundlis to determine past, present, and future life events for the individual. It also tells them about what makes that individual who they are, such as their preferences, spiritual inclination, and much more. In short, it provides information on just about every aspect of your life, current and past. It isn't difficult to read a kundli; you just need to understand certain things first. This chapter will show you how to decode your own birth chart.

The Importance of a Kundli

Kundlis can determine your life issues and how to deal with them.
https://pixabay.com/id/vectors/bagan-astrologi-veda-perbintangan-7156516/

A Kundli helps a person understand issues they may have in their life and deal with them. It also provides certain solutions and remedies to some of your challenges.

Here are some of the reasons why a kundli is so important:

1. A Kundli can be used for prospective relationships and marriages. The horoscopes of both parties are compared to ensure they are a good match. In Hinduism, a marriage cannot take place if the Kundlis do not match. The chart will also reveal certain details about married life, the partner, your mutual understanding, and possible challenges you may face.
2. A Kundli also tells us of difficulties ahead in our lives, not to mention opportunities that may arise, and it will tell us what kind of obstacles we are likely to face and how we should handle negative times.
3. A Kundli analyzes what makes you who you are; your personality, traits, and characteristics. In short, it tells you who you are, inside and out.
4. A Kundli can tell you your potential for wealth, how your business and career path will pan out, and whether you might be involved in business ventures in the future. It can tell you whether circumstances will be in your favor when you need to make economic decisions.
5. A Kundli can also provide details of your health – now and future – and your future family life. It will also indicate your academics, whether anyone is against you, and your creativity. You can understand the potential success, or otherwise, of your life, your health factor, and more.

Let's dive into the steps you must follow to decode your Kundli.

Determine Your Lagna or Ascendant

This is the exact time and place you were born.

Your Lagna is your Rising Sign, the zodiac sign that rose on the Eastern horizon at the time of your birth. As you already know, the sky is split into 12 equal parts of 30 degrees each, one for each sign. Your ascendant is also 30 degrees, and it tells you what was going on when you were born and what you might be in the future. It will also indicate ways to learn from life's lessons and apply them to learn more or teach others.

Calculating your Rising Sign manually is difficult, and it's best left to a professional astrologer. Alternatively, you can use one of the many free online calculators but do make sure you use a reputable one. Whichever method you choose, you will need certain information to hand in.

You will need to know the exact time you were born and the exact place. This is your Lagna or Ascendant, and that is why you really do need to know the exact time you were born and the exact place. If you don't know your exact time, 12 noon is typically used, which may, though, cause inaccuracies in the chart.

Rising Signs or Ascendants in Astrology

In Vedic astrology, an individual's Lagna tells much about their personality. On your birth chart, the Rising Sign is placed in the center, in the first House. The first house is all about how you look physically, what you do and don't like, what your childhood was like, and any strengths or weaknesses you have. It also indicates how you will see your life, attitude, behavior, and much more. Every Lagna has an element that tells you even more about who you are.

Rising Sign Elements

Every zodiac, or Rashi, also has an element, and you can see which signs are associated with which element below:

- **Air Signs:** Gemini, Libra, Aquarius
- **Earth Signs:** Taurus, Virgo, Capricorn
- **Fire Signs:** Aries, Leo, Sagittarius
- **Water Signs:** Cancer, Scorpio, Pisces

To add to these, each Lagna also has a ruling planet. The chart below shows the effects the ruling planets and elements have on your life and how your characteristics are defined:

RISING SIGN	SYMBOL	RULING PLANET	CHARACTERISTICS
Aries	♈ Ram	♂ Mars	Boldness Optimism Passion Outspokenness
Taurus	♉ Bull	♀ Venus	Ambition Smart Trustworthy Determined
Gemini	♊ Twins	☿ Mercury	Curious Youthful Fun-loving Enthusiastic
Cancer	♋ Crab	☽ Moon	Caring Sensitive Matriarchal Dependent
Leo	♌ Lion	☉ Sun	Creative Extroverted Confident Dominant
Virgo	♍ Virgin	☿ Mercury	Smart Perfectionist Kind Sophisticated

RISING SIGN	SYMBOL	RULING PLANET	CHARACTERISTICS
Libra	♎ Scales	♀ Venus	Calculating Cool Charming Cerebral
Scorpio	♏ Scorpion	♂ Mars	Passionate Deep Secretive Mysterious
Sagittarius	♐ Archer	♃ Jupiter	Curious Wise Restless Explorer
Capricorn	♑ Sea-goat	♄ Saturn	Sincere Hard-working Soft-hearted Calm
Aquarius	♒ Water bearer	♄ Saturn	Charming Enchanting Humanitarian Sociable
Pisces	♓ Fish	♃ Jupiter	Creative Rigid Detached Generous

Rising Sun Degree

The degree of the Ascendant indicates how intense your Rising Sign's influence will be on your personality and life. Let's say your Rising Sign's degree is low. In that case, you will have very few of the characteristics associated with that sign. By contrast, a higher degree means you'll have more of them, and your character will be more strongly affected, be it positively or negatively. However, this mustn't be taken at face value; instead, it must be added to everything else that comes out of your birth chart.

The Difference Between Your Ascendant, Moon, and Sun Signs

First, the Sun's position at birth indicates what your Sun sign is. The Sun stays in each zodiac sign for around 30 days, which is why the signs are typically based on your birthdate. Most of the horoscopes you read in the papers or online use the Sun signs, which is why they are often vague. When you know your exact birth time, you know your Ascendant, which means predictions are made more accurately.

Your Moon sign is the sign the Moon was positioned in when you were born. The Moon remains in each sign for two to three days, which means these horoscopes are far more accurate than Sun sign horoscopes.

Your Ascendant may not be the same sign as the Moon was in when you were born. Because this changes so frequently, Rising Sun horoscopes are the most accurate.

The 12 Houses and the Ruler Planets

There are 12 houses in a birth chart in Vedic astrology, each representative of a certain life area. There is a ruling planet associated with each House, and these ruling planets are classified as Good, Bad, or Neutral. Their classification depends on a few factors, including the zodiac signs, the planet's rules, where it is placed, and its aspects. On top of that, each House is classified into one of three groups: Cardinal/Kendra, Fixed/Panapara, and Cadent/Apoklima.

Below you can see a chart showing each House, its ruling planet, classification, and an interpretation:

House	Ruling Planet	Classification	Interpretation
First - Lagna	☉ - Sun	Cardinal/Kendra	Self Personality Approach to life Physical appearance
Second	♃ - Jupiter (traditional) ♀ - Venus (Alternative)	Fixed/Panapara	Finances Values Possessions Family Speech
Third	♂ - Mars	Cadent/Apoklima	Siblings Communication Courage Short journeys Skills
Fourth	☾ - Moon	Kendra/Cardinal	Family Home Mother Roots Emotional wellbeing
Fifth	♃ - Jupiter (traditional) ☉ - Sun (alternative)	Fixed/Panapara	Children Creativity Romance Intelligence Education

House	Ruling Planet	Classification	Interpretation
Sixth	♂ - Mars	Cadent/Apoklima	Work Health Enemies Obstacles Service
Seventh	♀ - Venus	Cardinal/Kendra	Marriage Partnerships Marriage Open enemies Business
Eighth	♄ - Saturn	Fixed/Panapara	Longevity Hidden matters Occult Inheritances Transformation
Ninth	♃ - Jupiter	Cadent/Apoklima	Philosophy Long journeys Higher education Luck Spirituality
Tenth	♄ - Saturn	Cardinal/Kendra	Reputation Career Public image Social status Authority

House	Ruling Planet	Classification	Interpretation
Eleventh	♃ - Jupiter (traditional) ♄ - Saturn (alternative)	Fixed/Panapara	Social network Gains Friends Income Aspirations
Twelfth	♄ - Saturn (traditional) ♃ - Jupiter (alternative)	Cadent/Apoklima	Hidden entities Interpretation Endings Subconscious Isolation

In terms of the classification of the planets, they are as follows:

House	Sanskrit Name	Classification
First	Lagna Bhava	Neutral to Good
Second	Dhana Bhava	Good
Third	Sahaj Bhava	Neutral
Fourth	Sukha Bhava	Good
Fifth	Putra Bhava	Good
Sixth	Roga Bhava	Good to Bad
Seventh	Kalatra Bhava	Neutral to Good
Eighth	Mrityu Bhava	Bad

House	Sanskrit Name	Classification
Ninth	Bhagya Bhava	Good
Tenth	Karma Bhava	Good
Eleventh	Labha Bhava	Good
Twelfth	Vyaya Bhava	Bad

The Negative and Positive Aspects

The next step is identifying and analyzing the planets' negative and positive aspects. When you do this in Vedic astrology, some aspects are considered negative, while others are considered positive. Let's look at these in a little more detail:

Positive Aspects:
1. **Conjunction - 0° Aspect:** when two planets are close to one another, they combine their energies, and each strengthens the other's effects. In the areas these planets govern, this can result in more intensity and better focus.
2. **Trine - 120° Aspect:** when three planets form a trine aspect, the resulting energy flow is harmonious. This promotes creativity, ease, and positive developments in all areas governed by the planets.
3. **Sextile - 60° Aspect:** this aspect represents possibilities and opportunities, fostering productivity, cooperation, and growth. This allows balanced working between the involved planets.

Negative Aspects:
- **Opposition - 180° Aspect:** this aspect indicates challenges and tension. When planets are in opposition, it creates opposing forces and conflicts, requiring individuals to make changes in the affected areas or find a balance.
- **Square - 90° Aspect:** this aspect is all about conflict, obstacles, and internal struggles. When planets are in a square aspect, it can lead to challenges and friction, which need to be overcome using

resolution, determination, and effort.
- **Quincunx – 150° Aspect –** this aspect suggests adjustment and unease, indicating that the individual needs to compromise and adapt to ensure the planet's energies are reconciled.

Major Aspects

Here's a more in-depth look at how the Major Aspects affect your life:

Conjunction

Conjunctions occur when two planets are near each other, usually sharing a sign with only a few degrees separating them. Their energy joins forces when this happens, strengthening each planet's effects, creating a positive partnership. Astro weather is linked with the transit of the planets, indicating an increase in power on a day when the energy from two planets is blended. Transiting astrology also tells us that conjunctions are a sign of new beginnings. For example, when the Moon and Sun are in conjunction, it forms a New Moon. If that conjunction is visible on your Kundli, you were born under one of two astrological events: a solar eclipse or a New Moon; this means you will find it easier to keep your conscious and subconscious coordinated as you go after your current life goals.

Sextile

A sextile is an aspect that comes about when 60 degrees separate a pair of planets; that means there are two Rashis between them; this is considered a pleasant aspect. Both planets are in elements that complement each other, for example, Fire/Air or Earth/Water. This means the flow between them is easy, and they provide support for one another. Sextiles are resourceful, adaptable, versatile, and proactive people who always try to keep things harmonious. When a Sextile occurs, provided we go for it and put the work in, we may be able to take advantage of new opportunities. For example, if Neptune and Venus are sextiles in your birth chart, it indicates you are creative and romantic. Suppose the planets are in Sextile on seemingly random days. In that case, a person is likely to be more open-minded and open-hearted, usually drawn to beauty, romance, and art.

Square

In this aspect, three zodiac signs exist between two planets, each approximately 90 degrees apart. This is battle time, as each planet lines up for a fight. These planets typically share a type of sign, i.e., they are both fixed, cardinal, or mutable. To be fair, this is all they have; they have no other commonalities. Because the two planets are in disagreement, this aspect typically brings conflict or tension, and the only way out is some kind of compromise. For example, Saturn and Mars show up on your birth chart in a Square aspect; this means you usually feel like everyone is against you and that you are under constant criticism for everything you do. According to transiting astrology, on the days when Saturn and Mars are in this aspect, you should expect obstacles and frustration. However, although this might seem negative, these challenges can offer the most rewards; they teach you how to find your strengths and produce solutions.

Trine

A trine is an aspect that happens when 120 degrees separates a pair of planets; this means there are four Rashis between them. Both planets have the same element, too. This aspect brings luck, opportunities, and plenty of harmony, making it easier to move forward in life; typically, opportunities will present themselves everywhere you go, with no real effort on your part. However, this can cause laziness; where the square aspect forces you to work at getting what you want, the trine hands it to you on a plate. For example, your birth chart shows Mercury and Uranus in a trine. This indicates a quick-thinking, mentally agile person who is adaptable, open-minded, original, and creative. They are unconventional thinkers but excellent at communication. Days when this trine happens are likely to be good ones – days that make your creativity and open-mindedness join forces and shine.

Opposition

An opposition occurs when 180 degrees separate a pair of planets; that means they face each other. The opposite signs can be seen below:
- Aries/Libra
- Taurus/Scorpio
- Gemini/Sagittarius
- Cancer/Capricorn
- Leo/Aquarius
- Virgo/Pisces

This opposition may bring union and balance via compromise, almost as if the planets are two opposing puzzle pieces that fit together. However, it can also present obstacles. The planetary elements are compatible, for example, Earth/Water or Fire/Air. This shows that they can join forces if they want to. However, because they share a sign type, i.e., fixed/cardinal/mutable, they are somewhat stubborn, and moving them is like trying to move heaven and earth. Let's say the Moon and the Sun are in opposition; it could mean that the Sun is in Aries while the Moon is in Libra. This creates a push-pull between Aries' individual, self-assertive nature and Libra's harmonious nature (focused on relationships). In transiting astrology, the Sun's conscious self-expression and the Moon's emotional needs interact, bringing some tension but providing insight into underlying emotional patterns. It can also affect relationships but allows you to bring harmony and balance back into your life.

Minor Aspects

Now let's turn to the minor aspects. These are not so pronounced but still provide decent insight; they are usually more mental, spiritual, or emotional in their effects on you.

Inconjunct/Quincunx

These aspects usually lead to a sense of uneasiness. An inconjunct happens when a pair of planets are separated by about 150 degrees. The relationship between them is challenging but subtle, sometimes leading to no small amount of discomfort. Undoubtedly, one of these planets will have more dominant, stronger energy than the other.

Integration is needed, and working with these inconjuncts will need patience and a willingness to find the right path forward. However, because the two energies are not fluid in their integration, this is not going to be easy. You could think of this aspect as a time when you needed balance in your life and had to be creative in how you achieved it. To be fair, these planets have no commonalities, so this will be difficult to do, but perseverance pays its own dividends.

Quintile

A quintile aspect is about accessing your talents and heightened senses, creating a feel-good vibe. However, it won't just happen. You need to make it work. Quintiles happen when there are 72 degrees between two planets; a birth chart will show it as a circle containing a five-point star. Quintiles make you more ambitious, allowing you to make an impact and truly be yourself. They also let us see things from a different perspective that others do not perceive.

Semi-Sextile

A semi-sextile comes about when 30 degrees separate a pair of planets, and this can lead to a gentle, attractive flow of energy between them. This tells us that the planets are interested in each other, but much work is needed for anything to come of it. The planets are in zodiac signs next to one another, and succeeding or preceding signs are usually different, not sharing anything, including modalities, elements, or polarities. Semi-sextile planets are in adjacent zodiac signs and zodiac signs that precede. They cannot see one another, making them feel somewhat strange, but we can gain something from semi-sextiles. This is an opportunity to work together to get the best out of a specific situation. While there is potential for understanding, it won't automatically happen. However, the risk of miscommunication can be avoided, provided you are aware of it.

Semi-Square

These two planets are side-eying one another. They are linked at a 45-degree angle in signs or houses that are next to one another. There isn't so much tension as the square aspect provides, but there is still the potential for that tension to fray your nerves a little. The trick is to ground yourself and stay balanced and calm. Otherwise, you won't get through the energy. Be aware of how you respond to tension or conflict so you can make the best choices to keep things ticking over smoothly.

Sesquiquadrate/Sesquisquare

This aspect happens when 135 degrees separates two planets and creates a cranky energy. Neither planet wants to work with the other, creating some subtle tension. The only real way to deal with this is to face it down honestly. Don't give in to conflict; instead, exercise control and moderation. Working through this is better than being stubborn all your life.

Analyze the Yogas and Doshas

To do this, you need to study certain alignments and/or combinations of planets in your birth chart. These will have a specific influence on your life and are highly significant to you. What are they? Read on, and you'll find out.

Here's how to analyze them:

1. **Study The Planetary Combinations:** Look for the combinations of planets that form the doshas and yogas in your birth chart. To do

this, look at the planet's placements, aspects, conjunctions, and strength.
2. **Understand the Yogas:** Yogas are favorable planet combinations, indicating benefits or strengths in certain areas of your life. Every yoga has its own impacts and characteristics, so when you identify your yogas, study their effects to see their influence over areas of your life like spirituality, health, career, wealth, and so on.
3. **Interpret the Doshas:** Doshas are not-so-favorable planet combinations that indicate obstacles or challenges in your life and often represent negative influences or Karmic imbalances. When you identify your doshas, study them to identify their effects on your life. Be aware that doshas aren't necessarily indicators of doom, nor are they definitely negatives. They can also teach you how to grow and provide you with opportunities to do so.
4. **Think about Dignity and Strength:** Assess each planet's dignity and strength. A well-placed strong planet can wipe out the doshas' negative effects and reinforce the yogas' positive effects. Conversely, weak planets can make the doshas' challenges seem much bigger and weaken the yogas' positive influences.
5. **Look at the House Placements:** Look at the houses in the positions of the yogas and doshas. These give you insight into the areas of your life these planetary combinations influence. Think about the natural implications of each house and their interaction with the combinations to determine their effects on you and your life.
6. **Ask for Help:** You need to understand Vedic astrology to interpret yogas and doshas, so consider asking a professional astrologer with plenty of experience to help you understand their significance.

Everyone has a unique birth chart, and you should analyze the yogas and doshas holistically, making sure you consider other factors, such as planetary positions.

Analyze the Nakshatras and Dashas

This requires understanding how the Dashas (planetary periods) and Nakshatras (lunar mansions) influence your life. Analyze them in the following way:

1. **Identify the Nakshatra:** Work out which one the Moon was positioned in at your time of birth. As you already know, each Nakshatra has a ruling deity, characteristics, and symbolism. Study the traits and qualities associated with your particular Nakshatra to understand your tendencies, personality, and potential themes throughout your life.
2. **Assess the Nakshatra's Lord:** These were mentioned in the chapter on Nakshatras; these are the planets or lords of the Moon's Nakshatra at your time of birth. The lord influences your behavior, emotional wellbeing, and life experiences. Study their aspects, strength, position, and condition to understand their impact on your life.
3. **Interpret the Nakshatra Padas:** Every Nakshatra is divided into four equal quarters called a Pada. These give you more insight into certain areas of your life, such as personal growth, spirituality, relationships, etc. Look at the Pada, where the important planets are positioned, to learn more about certain influences and outcomes related to those areas.
4. **Study the Dashas:** A Dasha is a planetary period that unfolds at certain times in your life. Find the current Dasha periods and subperiods, called Bhuktis, to determine which planetary energies are dominant at any given time. Study the nature of the planets in the Dashas and their implications, and work out how they influence certain areas of your life throughout those periods. Pay close attention to important experiences or events that occur with certain Dashas.
5. **Consider the Dasha Interactions:** Look at how the Dashas for different plants interact and analyze their relationships. Some will complement one another and create good times, while others will almost certainly clash, causing many challenges. Study the Dashas to determine their sequence and duration to gain insight into the trajectory of your life and each period's associated experiences and themes.
6. **Ask for Help:** Again, interpreting these is not easy for a beginner, so ask for help from a professional astrologer to help you understand the significance of the Dashas and Nakshatras in your birth chart.

Dashas and Nakshatras are integral in Vedic astrology, and being able to analyze them provides a deeper understanding of your birth chart. The Dashas' cyclical nature and the Nakshatras' rich symbolism will tell you much about your life themes and the various stages you will go through.

Reading a Vedic Kundli

Let's wrap up with a quick look at how to read your own chart:

Determine Your Rising Sign

As you already know, this sign is the one in your first house when you were born. The number in each section, or house, represents the individual's Ascendant or Rising Sign. You can see below that we use ordinary numbers for the zodiac signs; if you see Roman numerals on your chart, they indicate the houses:

1 – Aries

2 – Taurus

3 – Gemini

4 – Cancer

5 – Leo

6 – Virgo

7 – Libra

8 – Scorpio

9 – Sagittarius

10 – Capricorn

11 – Aquarius

12 – Pisces

Understand Each House and Its Influence and Significance:

There are 12 houses, and each shows up in an individual's birth chart; each one is related to an aspect of you and your life. This means that each planet or sign in a house will have some influence on how that house affects you. You know that the Roman numerals denoted the houses in the above chart; here's what they are:

Roman Numeral	House	Representation
I	First House	Self Physical traits and features Personality Characteristics
II	Second House	Primary Knowledge Wealth Family Finances
III	Third House	Skills Communication Younger siblings Efforts Hobbies
IV	Fourth House	Mother Happiness Land Secondary education Property Vehicles
V	Fifth House	Creativity Higher education Love Affairs of the heart Wittiness Progeny Past-life experiences

Roman Numeral	House	Representation
VI	Sixth House	Profession Debt Advocacy Disease Enemies
VII	Seventh House	Marriage Long-term relationships Long-term partnerships Import/export Public image Spouse
VIII	Eighth House	Unexpected events Longevity Research
IX	Ninth House	Higher learning Beliefs Father Luck Religion Mentor Long-distance journeys
X	Tenth House	Karma/actions Profession Job Career

Roman Numeral	House	Representation
XI	Eleventh House	Income Ambition Gains Older siblings
XII	Twelfth House	Experience

Identify Your Birth Chart's Nine Planets

When you are born, your unique kundli takes a snapshot of the sky, showing the positioning of the constellations and planets at the exact time you enter the world. You need to understand the planets, the abbreviated names you will see on your chart, and their significance:

Planet	Abbreviation	Significance
Sun - ☉	Su	Ruler Energy source Life source King of all planets Masculine nature
Moon - ☾	Mo	Mind Inner self Intellect Good memory Fertility Feminine nature
Mercury - ☿	Me	Speech Communication Intellectual Witty Calculative

Planet	Abbreviation	Significance
Mars - ♂	Ma	Courage Passion Short-tempered Physically string Argumentative Younger siblings Daring
Venus - ♀	Ve	Materialistic pleasure Love Beauty Romance Marriage Music Friendship Art
Jupiter - ♃	Ju	Higher education Spirituality Research
Saturn - ♄	Sa	Land Property Misfortune Secret Sorrow Hard work Name/fame Prestige

Planet	Abbreviation	Significance
Rahu	Ra	Foreigners Grandparents Foreign travel Gambling Theft Yet-to-be-diagnosed health issues Finance Over-ambitious Loss of reputation
Ketu	Ke	Spiritual inclination Grandparents Electronics superstitions

Determine Planetary Exaltation and Debilitation

Next, work out which planets are in exaltation and debilitation. Exaltation is when one planet has stronger energy and qualities when it is in a certain Rashi. At this time, the planet is doing its best work and is at its most positive.

Conversely, debilitation is when the planet and sign are not in sync; rather, one agitates the other, weakening the planet's influence and providing a typically unfavorable outcome. The chart below shows all the details you need to know at a glance:

Planet	Ruling Sign	Exalted Sign	Debilitated Sign
Sun	Leo	Aries	Libra
Moon	Cancer	Taurus	Scorpio

Planet	Ruling Sign	Exalted Sign	Debilitated Sign
Venus	Taurus Libra	Pisces	Virgo
Mars	Aries Scorpio	Capricorn	Cancer
Saturn	Aquarius Capricorn	Libra	Aries
Jupiter	Sagittarius Pisces	Cancer	Capricorn
Mercury	Gemini Virgo	Virgo	Pisces
Rahu	N/A	N/A	N/A
Ketu	N/A	N/A	N/A

Being able to read and understand your Kundli will give you a general look at your life, but for a more detailed look and deeper insights, you should seek the guidance of an experienced astrologer.

Chapter 9: Astrological Remedies

Eleanor Roosevelt once said, *"Happiness is not a goal; it's a by-product of a life well-lived."* Most people live their lives constantly searching for happiness and peace and will do whatever is humanly possible to get things moving however they want. But there's more than what's humanly possible. Your life is ruled from above by the planets and their malefic and benefic positions in your birth charts. Simply put, an individual's deeds – good or bad – and their Karma and the planet's positions are important in setting their path in life.

Good Karma leads to a good, happy life, while bad Karma leads to a life filled with difficulty and issues in many areas of your life, such as finances, health, and more. As such, nothing is random about your life; everything that happens is predefined due to planetary, house, and sign placements when you are born.

Vedic astrology tells you that the planets in your birth chart may be benefic, i.e., they resonate with positive energy and bring positive effects into your life, or they may be malefic, which means they bring negativity and bad effects. They may also be neutral, which means they bring neither good nor bad energy. Vedic astrology also tells you that there are some remedies you can use to remove malefic signs. These remedies can improve your life by wiping out the malefic planet's negative effects.

Gemstone therapy is a form of astrological remedy.
https://unsplash.com/photos/1Vd5b63876g?utm_source=unsplash&utm_medium=referral&utm_content=creditShareLink

There are many different types of remedies, the two most notable being Vedic (those passed down through time) and Contemporary (formulated with the world in the current scenario in mind). As you will discern, some remedies are relatively new concepts and wouldn't have been done in the past simply because certain places and things didn't exist. Examples are donating money, goods, or time to a nursing home or orphanage.

Why Remedies Are Effective

Remedies are simply solutions for antitoxins, except these are magical, mysterious clairvoyant antitoxins. These solutions eliminate, or at least dilute, the effects bad past Karma has brought to your current life. By now, you should understand that what you did in your past lives affects your current life.

A remedy is a process by which you do something or refrain from doing something you have gotten into the habit of doing. Some remedies are Vedic, which means they have been done through the eras, while others are relatively new.

Before looking at some remedies, you need to understand what people have been doing for many years, so here are some of the common remedies that people practice:

Gemstone Therapy:

Gemstones are thought to harness energy from certain planets, channeling it into the life of the person who uses the gemstone. Every stone is associated with a certain planet, and wearing or using it can enhance its beneficial aspects while eliminating the malefic effects.

Gemstones are usually chosen based on an individual's planetary influences, as shown in their birth chart. For instance, blue sapphire is associated with Saturn, and wearing it can bring wealth, stability, and discipline, while Ruby is associated with the Sun and can strengthen leadership qualities and vitality.

Mantra Chanting:

A mantra is a sacred phrase or sound repeated to induce a certain vibration. You can bring positive energy and balance to your life if you chant a mantra that is related to a certain planet or deity. Every planet has different mantras, which can be chanted as little or as often as needed to appease them, and they are powerful, resonating with certain frequencies from the planet.

The "Om Namah Shivaya" mantra is chanted to reduce or eliminate the negative effects coming from Mars and is associated with Lord Shiva, while the "Om Brihaspataye Namaha" appeases Jupiter.

Chanting mantras regularly is thought to provide spiritual benefits, purify the mind, and align the individual with the planet's energies.

Yantra Meditation:

A yantra is a geometric diagram that represents planets or deities. Meditating on one is thought to help you focus your mind and align your energy with that of the particular planet or deity the yantra represents. Yantras are used a lot in meditation and to help a person to bring positive influences into their lives.

Vedic Rituals and Homas:

Vedic rituals, also called pujas or yagyas, revolve around performing a ceremony and making an offering to a planetary force or deity. Qualified astrologers or priests typically perform them, and it is thought they appease the influences from specific planets and bring good luck and blessings to the individual.

The rituals and homas are quite complex and usually comprise prayers, fire ceremonies, and offerings to appease the planets. A homa is a fire ritual where sacred materials such as herbs and ghee are offered while a mantra is recited. The offerings are made into a consecrated fire.

The rituals are believed to help bring harmony between the energies and allow the planets and deities to send blessings.

Donations and/or Charitable Acts:

It is thought that when a person donates money, items, or time or carries out a charitable act, it can wipe out negative Karma and appease the malefic influences. Most often donated are money, food, clothing, and other necessary items to those less fortunate, hoping to eliminate the negative influences.

Giving something back through charity is considered honorable in some cultures, and it's believed these things generate positive energies and bring balance and harmony to your life.

Fasting:

Fasting is commonly followed in many religions and cultures. In terms of astrology, it is said that a person can reduce a planet's negative influences by fasting on days associated with that planet. For example, fast on a Saturday if you need to appease Saturn, on a Tuesday to appease Mars, or on a Thursday to appease Jupiter.

Fasting is a form of purification and self-discipline, and it helps clean the mind and body and provides a stronger connection to the divine energies.

Astrological Remedial Objects:

Gemstones are not the only objects a person can use for astrological remedies. There are plenty of others available, such as amulets and talismans. These are thought to have a protective energy and are usually kept somewhere personal or worn. Rudraksha beads are made from Rudraksha tree seeds and are usually worn as bracelets or necklaces; they are associated with wellbeing and spiritual growth.

The object a person uses is based on their astrological requirements and will provide protection and enhance positive energy.

One important thing to be aware of is that astrological remedies are entirely subjective, based purely on your needs and beliefs. Some people find great comfort when they follow astrological remedies and believe it brings positive changes to their lives. However, you should consult with a qualified astrologer or Vedic practitioner before you start using them.

When Is the Right Time for Remedies?

One of the most important parts of using astrological remedies is choosing the right time to do it. The remedy's effectiveness is influenced by several factors, including the planets' positions at certain times. Here are some things you should consider when choosing the right time:

1. **Planetary Hours:** each planet is associated with planetary hours, which are specific hours in the day. These are based on the time of sunrise and sunset, and choosing the hour that aligns with the planet you want to strengthen or appease can make the remedy more effective. For instance, if you are chanting a mantra to Jupiter, choose the right planetary hour but be aware that this changes daily.

2. **Auspicious Days:** some planets have favorable or auspicious days, for example, Tuesday for Mars, Thursday for Jupiter, etc. The positive effects will be considerably enhanced if you choose auspicious days to perform your rituals or remedies for a planet. You may need to get help from an astrologer to determine the right days for each remedy.

3. **Planetary Transits:** this indicates the planetary movement through each zodiac sign and can have a big influence over when you do your remedies. When a planet is moving through a favorable position or sign, that is a good time for the remedies related to that planet. For example, suppose Venus is in Libra (its own sign). In that case, it is a good time for remedies related to Venus, such as performing harmony or love rituals.

4. **Personal Birth Chart:** your birth chart is one of the biggest indicators of when the time is right for remedies. Where the planets are positioned at the time of your birth must be considered alongside the current planetary transits and progressions. Again, seek advice from an experienced astrologer to find the right time.

5. **Muhurta Selection:** Muhurta is another way of referencing the auspicious time for remedies and other astrological activities. Muhurta selection requires you to study the positions of the planets and identify their influences to work out the best time for the remedy. This can include things like how the benefic planets are aligned, a lack of malefic influence, and the favorable conditions of the right time.

Strengthening the Planets

In Vedic astrology, every individual's life is ruled over by nine planets. If all nine planets are strong in an individual's birth chart, that person will be strong enough to fight whatever life throws their way. Each planet plays a role in human life. When a planet is in a weak position in the horoscope, its effect will be experienced in many ways throughout life. For example, the individual will lack abilities and fortune, won't have a peaceful life, and won't be strong or stable.

You can't change your birth chart, but you can work toward strengthening the planets using remedies to appease them.

Doing so will require you to make changes in your routine, living, eating, and behavior, but using the following remedies can help you bring prosperity and peace to your life:

How to Strengthen the Sun:
- Every morning, spend some time sitting in the sunlight
- Eat your last meal of the day before the sun sets
- Drink your water from a copper vessel
- Only use wooden furniture
- Chant the Surya Mantra daily to energize your birth chart's planet

The Surya Mantra:
Namah Suryaya Shantaya Sarvaroga Nivaarine,

Ayurarogya Masivairyam Dehi Deva Jagapate.

The English translation is:

Surya Deva, Ruler of the Universe, you are the remover of all disease, the repository of peace. I bow to you, and please bless your devotees with long life, health, and wealth.

How to Strengthen the Moon:
- Change your diet. Eat fresh, whole foods and plenty of fruit. Do not eat cold foods at night
- Don't waste water

How to Strengthen Mars:
- Do not use negative words
- Avoid using an angry tone
- Think five times or more before you say something

- Chant the Hanuman Chalisa daily

The Hanuman Chalisa:

40 verses long, the Hanuman Chalisa is a devotional hymn, and the first and last verses are:

Shri Guru Charan Saroj Raj,
Nij Man Mukur Sudhari,
Barnau Raghubar Bimal Jasu,
Jo Dayaku Phal Chari.

Translated into English:

With the dust from the lotus feet of Sri Guru,
I clean the mirror of my mind and recite,
The pure glory of Lord Ram, the supreme among the Raghu dynasty,
Who bestows the four fruits of life.

And the last verse:

Pavan Tanay Sankat Haran,
Mangal Moorti Roop,
Ram Lakhan Sita Sahit,
Hriday Basahu Sura Bhoop

And the English translation:

O Hanuman, the son of the wind,
The remover of all sorrows, the embodiment of auspiciousness,
Reside in my heart, along with Lord Ram, Lakshman, and Sita,
The King of the Devas

How to Strengthen Buddha

- Eat more green vegetables daily
- Listen to good music
- Don't use cosmetic products all the time
- Bathe regularly and keep your surroundings clean

How to Strengthen Jupiter

- Respect your elders
- Don't get involved in gossip, idle or otherwise
- Use the color yellow – wear yellow clothes, have yellow belongings in your home, and use turmeric

How to Strengthen Venus:
- Respect the women in your family and life
- Avoid waste
- Eat plain yogurt daily
- Wear clean, bright clothing

How to Strengthen Rahu and Ketu
- To strengthen Rahu, avoid jealous feelings, and think and speak positively
- To strengthen Ketu, let go of the past and focus firmly on your future.

Health Remedies

Vedic astrology provides several health-related remedies, and the most common ones are:

1. **Worship Lord Dhanvantari and Make Appropriate Offerings:** Lord Dhanvantari is the deity of healing and health, and when you worship him and make appropriate offerings, including:
    - Fresh flowers, especially lotus
    - Burn incense, resins, or aromatic herbs
    - Light an oil lamp in front of a Lord Dhanvantari idol or image
    - Water offered in a conch shell or small vessel
    - Prasadam – blessed vegetarian food (no garlic or onion)
    - Tulsi leaves – holy basil
    - Recite the Dhanvantari mantra

Dhanvantari Mantra:

Om Namo Bhagavate Vasudevaya Dhanvantaraye

Amritakalasha Hastaya Sarvamaya Vinashanaya

Trilokya Nathaya Shri Mahavishnave Namaha

English Translation:

Salutations to the Divine Lord Vasudeva (another name for Lord Vishnu) and Lord Dhanvantari,

Who holds the pot of nectar in his hands,

The destroyer of all ailments and diseases,

The Lord of the three worlds (physical, astral, and causal),

I bow down to the great Lord Vishnu

2. **Ayurvedic Practices:** Ayurveda is the ancient Indian medicine system that works closely with Vedic astrology. Your health will flourish when you include Ayurvedic practices in your life and follow Ayurvedic principles. This includes eating a healthy, balanced diet per your specific body type, regular yoga and/or exercise, and using Ayurvedic remedies and herbs where needed.

3. **Offering or Donating Food/Money/Items:** Donating to those less fortunate than you is considered a very powerful remedy. Any selfless act brings positive energy to your life and adds to your wellbeing. Donations of food to orphanages, hospitals, and food kitchens or participating in a food drive in your community can benefit your mental and physical health.

4. **Chanting Mantras:** Chanting mantras specific to health and wellbeing can effectively boost your health. Three of the most common are the Dhanvantari Mantra, the Maha Mrityunjaya Mantra, and the Gayatri Mantra, and chanted regularly with pure intention and devotion, they can positively impact your mental and physical health.

5. **Performing Yagya or Homa:** As you learned above, these sacred fire rituals invoke various deities' blessings. You can perform health-related yagyas or homas, such as Maha Mrityunjaya Yagya or Ayushya Homa, to ensure good health and ask for divine intentions. However, rituals like these are typically performed by experienced astrologers or priests.

6. **Planetary Remedies:** Specific planets are associated with health and all related matters in Vedic astrology. If a specific planet on your birth chart is giving you trouble in the health department, you can use remedies to strengthen it. This could include specific rituals or wearing gemstones associated with that planet.

You must note that Vedic astrological remedies are not to be substituted for professional treatment. If you have a serious medical condition or are feeling unwell, you should also seek medical advice.

Career Remedies

1. **Worship Lord Ganesha:** Lord Ganesha is considered the remover of obstacles and the deity of success and wisdom. Lord Ganesha should be worshipped before you head off to a new job or change your professional path in life; this will help bring you blessings and eliminate the obstacles in your way. Regular offerings of incense, flowers, and sweets should be made to Lord Ganesha regularly, along with your most sincere prayers.

2. **Chanting Mantras:** Choose a mantra associated with success and growth in your career, as these are said to be incredibly beneficial. Some of the most common are the Navagraha Mantra, Saraswati Mantra, and the Gayatri Mantra, all recited to help enhance professional skills, knowledge, and success. Chanting these regularly with devotion and focus will bring new opportunities and positive energy.

3. **Offer the Sun Some Water:** In Vedic astrology, the sun represents power, authority, and career growth. When you offer water to the Sun at sunrise while reciting the Surya Mantra or Gayatri Mantra is considered to bring luck in career advancement. It is believed to invoke the Sun's positive energies and boost your career prospects.

4. **Donating/Charitable Actions:** When you carry out acts of compassion or charity, you create good Karma, which in turn impacts favorably on your professional life. The best charitable acts are donating to educational institutions, participating in skill development-related community service projects, and supporting less fortunate people.

5. **Yantra for Success:** You already know that a yantra is a geometric diagram and a mantra associated with a specific planetary influence or deity. For example, the Sri Yantra is powerful for prosperity and success. Energizing a Sri Yantra and placing it in your workplace or putting a small one in your pocket or bag can boost your career growth and positive vibrations.

6. **Perform a Navagraha Puja:** This ritual is dedicated to the nine planets and involves prayers and rituals designed to balance and appease the planetary influences over your professional career. This type of ritual is usually carried out by a qualified astrologer who will guide you through the ritual based on your needs and

planetary positions.

7. **Gemstone Therapy:** It is known that gemstones carry positive energies when used in the right way. Wearing or using gemstones associated with the planets related to career and professional life - Saturn (blue Sapphire) or the Sun (Ruby) will help enhance your professional growth. Choose the right gemstones based on your specific birth chart.

Practice your remedies with faith, sincerity, dedication, and hard work. They are not a cure-all; rather, they are intended to enhance and support your efforts.

Relationships/Marriage

1. **Worship the Goddess Parvati and Lord Shiva:** The Lord and Goddess are the divine couple, representing harmony in marriage and long-term relationships. When you worship them, do so with devotion and offer prayers to help you fix problems in your marriage. A couple may do a joint ritual or ceremony, seeking blessings from Lord Shiva and Goddess Parvati for a long, loving, harmonious relationship.

2. **Chanting Mantras:** There are some mantras specific to harmony, love, and married bliss, and chanting them can provide help. The two most commonly recited are the Swayamvara Parvathi and Om Namah Shivaya mantras, both attracting love and helping strengthen the bond between the people in the relationship. Chanting these regularly, alone or as a couple, can bring positivity to the marriage.

3. **Observe Vrat:** This means to fast; doing it on certain days associated with harmony in a relationship or marriage brings positive vibrations. The Karva Chauth vrat is typically done by married women and is dedicated to ensuring the longevity and wellbeing of their husbands. Fasting on the right day will strengthen the bond between you.

4. **Perform a Navagrah Puja:** As mentioned earlier, this is a ritual dedicated to the planets. When you conduct it, make sure your focus is on making the benefic planets associated with relationships and marriage stronger - this includes Jupiter and Venus. Doing so will eliminate or reduce many marital problems.

5. **Wear Gemstones:** Gemstones associated with the relationship planets, i.e., Jupiter (yellow Sapphire) and Venus (Diamond), are recommended to improve harmony in your marriage. These gemstones boost positive energies surrounding understanding, commitment, and love.
6. **Seek Astrological Help:** Seek guidance from an experienced astrologer to gain insight into what might be causing the problems in your marriage or relationship. They will examine your birth chart and recommend specific remedies, such as those mentioned above, once they have analyzed the planets and their influence and impact on your relationship.

Love Life

1. **Worship Lord Kamadeva:** The Vedic deity of desire and love, you should worship Lord Kamadeva with devotion and offer prayers to help bring love to your life or enhance a current romantic liaison. Regularly offer prayers or perform rituals to seek Lord Kamadeva's blessings for a loving relationship.
2. **Chant Mantras:** Some mantras are associated with romance and love; chanting them can bring love and positive vibrations into your life. Two of the most commonly recited are the Kamadeva Gayatri and the Kleem mantras, used to invoke love's energy. Chant them regularly with sincerity and focus to bring improvements to your love life.
3. **Enhance Your Venus Energy:** Venus is the planet of beauty, romance, and love, according to Vedic astrology. When you strengthen this planet's energy, it can benefit your love life significantly. To do this, wear gemstones associated with Venus, such as a Diamond, White Topaz, or White Sapphire, and you can also add pastel shades, pink, or white colors to your wardrobe to bring on a romantic atmosphere.
4. **Perform a Navagraha Puja:** Worshipping the nine planets can bring harmony and balance to the planetary energies influencing your love life. More specifically, you should pay close attention to where Venus and Mars are placed in your birth chart, and their influences can help you perform the Navagraha Puja to bring them into balance and strengthen them.

5. **Offer Flowers:** Identify the deities associated with relationships and love and offer them fresh flowers, specifically roses. Making these offerings to Goddess Lakshmi or Lord Krishna can enhance romance and love in your life. Make your offerings with devotion and prayer, and clearly express your desire to have a loving relationship.
6. **Practice Self-Care and Self-Love:** Both are critical to attracting and nurturing love in your life. Look after your emotional and physical wellbeing, do things that make you happy, and build a positive mindset. Be self-reflective and work hard on your personal growth; positive energy radiates when you practice self-love and will help you attract the right relationships.
7. **Seek Astrological Help:** Consult a Vedic astrologer to get insights into the planets and their influence over your love life. A professional astrologer will look at your birth chart, identify the planetary positions and any imbalances or hurdles, and recommend the right practices and remedies to help you.

Don't forget; for astrological remedies to work, you must be sincere in your efforts, open in your communication, and genuinely want connection and love.

This guide finishes with an important chapter – a glossary of terms to help you understand everything you read and hear about the lunar nodes and Vedic astrology.

Bonus Chapter: Glossary of Terms

Learning all about Vedic astrology and the lunar nodes is hard enough, but it's even tougher when you don't understand the definitions and terms used. Below you can find the most common terms you are likely to come across:

A

- **Akshavedamsa (*uhk-shah-veh-dahm-suh*):** better known as the D-45, this is one of the divisional or Varga divisional charts, sometimes called the Pancha-Chatvaryansh. It is used to help an astrologer determine insights into an individual's character and personality.
- **Amrita (*uhm-ree-tuh*):** is the "nectar of immortality," and it also refers to a time when the planetary influences are favorable, indicating positivity and harmony.
- **Artha (*ahr-thuh*):** represents wealth and prosperity, material pursuits, and practical and career matters.
- **Ascendant:** the sign on the Eastern horizon when a person is born, indicating your appearance and personality.
- **Ashtakavarga (*uhsh-tah-kah-vahr-guh*):** a system that analyzes the planets' strengths and weaknesses in your birth chart.
- **Aspect:** the influence of one planet directed at another in your chart.
- **Atma (*aht-muh*):** this represents the self, the universe's absolute reality.

- **Avasthas** (*uh-vahs-thahs*): in Vedic astrology, this indicates the conditions or states of the planets. It provides insight into how the planets behave in your birth chart, their activity, and their strength.
- **Ayanamsha** (*ah-yuh-nuhm-shuh*): the difference between the sidereal and tropical zodiacs in longitude.
- **Ayurveda** (*ah-yoor-veh-duh*): a natural medicine system in India.

B

- **Bala**: *(bah-luh):* this term is commonly used in Vedic astrology to describe a planet's power or strength. It represents the planet's inherent capacity to produce unfavorable or favorable effects based on its aspects and position.
- **Bhanga**: *(bahng-guh):* this is used to denote when a planetary yoga or combination is nullified or canceled. This happens when specific factors or conditions offset the potential or effects of a planetary combination, negating or diminishing the outcome.
- **Bhava** (*bahng-guh*): a birth chart has 12 bhava, or houses, each representing an aspect of an individual's life – wealth, career, personality, relationships, etc.
- **Bhukti** (*bhuhk-tee*): a period within a major period or dasha

C

- **Cardinal:** these four zodiac signs are the first ones for each season: Aries is spring, Cancer is summer, Libra is fall, and Capricorn is winter.
- **Chakra** (*chuh-kruh*): the body's energy centers, each with a specific influence from the planets
- **Chaturthamsa** (*chuh-tur-thahm-suh*): the D-4, this chart is also a Varga or divisional chart. An astrologer uses this one to determine an individual's fixed capital, moveable properties, and luck.
- **Chaturvishamsa** (*chuh-tur-vee-shahm-suh*): the D-10 is another divisional or Varga chart that an astrologer uses to determine an individual's learning, education, knowledge, and donation propensities throughout their life.
- **Chatvaryansh**: *(chuh-tvah-ryahn-shuh):* also called Chaturvimsamsa, this is one of the divisional charts used in Vedic

astrology. It separates a zodiac sign into 24 pieces, all the same size, each part representing a certain life area. It provides insight into an individual's potential, abilities, and skills in different domains.
- **Combustion:** describes a planet's condition when it is too near the Sun; that planet's significations are weakened.
- **Conjunction:** the energies from two or more planets in the same house are combined.
- **Cusp:** the invisible line separating two zodiac signs or houses next to each other in the birth chart.

D
- **Dasamsa (*duh-suhm-suh*):** the 10th divisional chart gives further insight into the individual's career path.
- **Dasha (*duhsha*):** planetary periods which divide an individual's life into separate periods, each section with a different planet ruler. An astrologer will analyze the timing and effects of each period to make predictions.
- **Dashmansh (*duhsh-muhn-shuh*):** the D-10 chart is different because it has nothing to do with the individual's lagna birth chart. Instead, it is used to determine details about an individual's current career path, possible careers for the future, and business and society goals.
- **Debilitation:** a planet in debilitation is in its weakest, most vulnerable position, potentially delivering negative effects.
- **Dharma (*duhr-muh*):** an individual's purpose and duty in life.
- **Divisional Chart:** divisional charts are separate, smaller birth charts used to provide additional insight into certain areas of an individual's life.
- **Dosha (*doh-shuh*):** this is a period of affliction or imbalance in a birth chart that can cause an individual some difficulties. The primary doshas are Kapha, Vata, and Pitta.
- **Drekkana (*dreh-kah-nuh*):** this chart contains the third-house affinities and relates to siblings.
- **Dreshkana (*drehsh-kah-nuh*):** the D-3 chart is a divisional/Varga chart that helps an astrologer determine information about an individual's hobbies and siblings. This links to the 3rd house,

which provides details about siblings, and the D-3 gives information about the 3rd house, the individual's courage, communication skills, siblings, and their actions to achieve their desires.

- **Drishti (*drish-tee*):** this is about how a planet projects its energy across the birth chart; it does this through its influence on the zodiac signs that it doesn't reside in.
- **Dusthana (*duhs-thah-nuh*):** the 6th, 8th, and 12th houses are collectively the dusthana, all with an association to some kind of suffering, i.e., the 6th house is associated with disease, the 8th with death, while the 12th house is associated with loss.
- **Dwadamsha (*dwah-duhm-shuh*):** one of the division charts; this gives more insight into previous lives, parents, heritage (ancestral), and past life Karma.
- **Dwara*: (dwuh-ruh):*** Dwara is the Sanskrit word for gateway or doorway. In astrology, it is used to refer to a specific sign or house's entry point or cusp in an individual's birth chart. It indicates a transition between different life areas and describes the energy flow between the two.

E

- **Ephemeris (*ih-feh-muh-ris*):** astrologers use this to work out birth charts and the movements of the planets.
- **Exaltation:** this indicates when a planet is manifesting its highest form of energy and is incredibly powerful.

F

- **Fixed:** the stable rashis who don't like change; the signs are Aquarius, Leo, Scorpio, and Taurus.

G

- **Gochara (*goh-chuh-ruh*):** this is the study of the planets' transit positions and how they affect individuals. The planetary movement is analyzed in relation to the birth chart's natal positions.
- **Graha Drishti (*gruh-huh- drish-tee*):** describes the aspect of a planet on another, referencing the influence one planet's position has on another or a specific house.

- **Graha (*gruh-huh*):** Sanskrit word meaning" planet." This includes celestial bodies we can all see, such as the Moon and Sun, and those we can't, like the lunar nodes (Rahu and Ketu).
- **Gyana*: (gyah-nuh):*** this Sanskrit word translates to wisdom or knowledge. In astrology, it refers to the intuitive insight and understanding that arises from metaphysical or spiritual knowledge. It also indicates a high level of enlightenment and consciousness.

H

- **Hora (*hoh-ruh*):** the 2nd divisional chart, connected to the 2nd house in a Rashi chart; Hora is related to wealth.
- **Horoscope:** a map or diagram indicating the positioning of the celestial bodies when a person was born; they are used to make predictions.
- **House:** the Zodiac is divided into 12, each called a house. Each influences a certain aspect of an individual's life.

J

- **Jaimini*: (jai-mih-nee):*** this refers to the astrology system called Jaimini, which was named after a sage called Jaomini Maharishi. It is an ancient tradition with its own techniques, principles, and chart interpretations. It focuses on certain planetary significations and aspects.
- **Jyotish (*jyoh-tish*):** the Sanskrit term that means astrology, specifically Vedic astrology
- **Jyotishi (*jyoh-tish-ee*):** an astrologer who uses the Vedic astrology system.

K

- **Kama (*kah-muh*):** represents passion and desire.
- **Kapha (*kah-fuh*):** an Ayurvedic energy or dosha that represents calm, stable qualities
- **Karaka (*kah-ruh-kuh*):** a planetary significator for certain life aspects.
- **Karma (*kahr-muh*):** an influence causing an effect, usually from actions in a previous life. Put simply, it's a case of what goes around, comes around; how you treat others and what you do in a past life will come back to you.

- **Kendra (*ken-druh*):** this represents the angular houses, which represent the most important life aspects and are significant; they are the 1st, 4th, 7th, and 10th houses. That said, planets in any of these houses will have a significant impact on an individual, but those in the 10th house are considered the most influential and should not be underestimated.
- **Ketu (*kay-too*):** the Moon's south node, created by Rahu's decapitation.
- **Khavadamsha (*khuh-vah-duhm-shuh*):** the D-40 chart is a Varga/divisional chart that an astrologer uses to determine an individual's auspicious/inauspicious results. It is also known as the Chatvaryansh.
- **Krishna Paksha *krihsh-nuh-puhk-shuh*):** the dark half of a month, also known as the waning Moon.
- **Kundli (*koon-dlee*):** Vedic name for birth chart.

L

- **Lagna (*luhg-nuh*):** the Ascendant, or the rising sign in an individual's birth chart. This is the planet that rise on the Eastern horizon when a person was born, and it determines their personality and how they look physically.
- **Lagna Lord:** the Lagna's ruling planet, this planet plays an important part in determining their influence and strength.
- **Lahiri*: (lah-hee-ree):* this refers to a popular Vedic ephemeris called the Lahiria Ephemeris. It offers precise positions for the planets and other data used for astrological calculations. This ephemeris is typically used to provide chart calculations and make accurate predictions.
- **Lajjitaadi*: (luh-jee-tah-dee):* this is a Vedic astrological term that describes a group of conditions (avasthas) that are credited to different planets. These avasthas represent the planets' dignities or states based on where they are laced in an individual's birth chart. They provide insight into the planet's behavior, strength, and effect on an individual's life.

M

- **Mahadasha (*muh-huh-dah-shuh*):** a Sanskrit word that translates to "major period." It is a planetary period that impacts an individual's life path for a set duration from the time of birth.

- **Mantra:** a sequence of words or sounds that provide vibration; used to appease the planets, these are usually used as astrological remedies.
- **Maraka (*muh-ruh-kuh*):** literally means "killer." However, it means death to health/longevity in astrology. The Maraka houses are the 2nd and 7th.
- **Moksha (*mohk-shuh*):** spiritual enlightenment and the concept of being released from the life/death cycle.
- **Moolatrikona (*moh-luh-trih-koh-nuh*):** a powerful degree range in a Rashi with a strong influence over a specific planet. Planets in moolatrikona are stronger than they are in their own sign but not as strong as when they are in exaltation.
- **Muhurta (*muh-hoor-tuh*):** choosing the right time to start a new venture or offer astrological remedies. Careful analysis must be done to choose the right time for the best outcomes.
- **Mutable:** the adaptable and variable zodiac signs. They are Gemini, Pisces, Sagittarius, and Virgo.

N

- **Nadi Astrology:** a Vedic astrology branch focused on predictions about an individual's past, present, and future. It uses manuscripts called Nadis, or palm leaves to make predictions and is typically practiced in Southern India.
- **Nakshatra (*nahk-shah-truh*):** the 27 constellations the zodiac is divided into are called the Lunar Mansions, or Nakshatras.
- **Nakshatra Dasha (*nahk-shah-truh-duh-shuh*):** planetary periods based on the Lunar Mansions; the system considers the Nakshatra sequence, including each one's ruling planet, to work out the effects and timing of different periods.
- **Nakshatra Lord:** each Nakshatra has a ruling planet known as the Lord. The Nakshatra Lord adds certain influences and qualities to the individual based on their unique birth chart.
- **Navagraha (*nuh-vuh-gruh-huh*):** the nine planets in a person's birth chart: Sun, Moor, Mars, Mercure, Jupiter, Venus, Saturn, Rahu, Ketu.
- **Navamsha (*nuh-vuhm-shuh*):** almost as important as the primary chart used in Vedic astrology, the navamsha is used in Western astrology and provides extra insight into long-term relationships.

It also helps determine whether a birth chart's indications will manifest easily or with difficulty. Some astrologers say the navamsha is the horoscope of the soul, and the Rashi represents other conditions in an individual's life.

- **Neecha-Bhanga Raj Yoga** (*nee-chuh-buhn-guh rahj yoh-guh*): a combination of planets that mitigate or cancel a specific planet's debilitation, bringing more positive effects, such as success, power, and wealth.
- **Nodes:** there are two shadow nodes attached to the Moon - Rahu (North) and Ketu (South). They cannot be seen, but they indicate the intersection of the ecliptic and the Moon as the Moon orbits, causing an eclipse.

P

- **Pakshala Bala** (*puhk-shuh-luh bah-luh*): this is when the strength of the Moon changes to a different cycle. Its strength changes throughout the Lunar month - usually called waxing (increasing) and waning (decreasing). Some astrologers say that when the Moon is fewer than 120 degrees away from the sun, it is weak. Conversely, it is considered strong when more than 120 degrees separate them.
- **Pancha: *(puhn-chuh):*** this Sanskrit word means five, and in Vedic astrology, it is used to describe the concept of the five fundamental principles or elements: Earth, Air, Water, Ether (space), and Fire. The elements are what the material world is built on; each has its own energies and qualities.
- **Panchang** (*puhn-chahng*): an almanac or calendar used to gain astrological information, such as planetary positions. This can be used to help an individual or astrologer determine the Muhurat to perform a specific task or remedy - that means finding the best time. The panchang has 5 limbs: Tithi (date), Nakshatra, Vaar (day), Karan, and Yog.
- **Pitta (*pih-tuh*):** the dosha in Ayurveda that the fire element rules.
- **Prakruti (*pruh-kroo-tee*):** a person's natural constitution; this is an indication of irritating doshas and weakness.
- **Prashna (*pruhsh-nuh*):** also called horary, this is an astrology branch revolving around answering questions using information from the time they were asked. At the time the question is asked,

an astrologer will analyze the chart.
- **Prishtodaya (*prish-toh-dah-yuh*)**: the signs rising in the East in the second part of a day – Aries, Cancer, Capricorn, Sagittarius, and Taurus.

R
- **Rahu (*rah-hoo*)**: the Moon's North Node
- **Rahu-Ketu**: the collective name for the North and South Nodes; Rahu and Ketu are shadow planets and are important celestial points with a huge impact on an individual's Karmic patterns and life.
- **Raja Yoga (*rah-juh yoh-guh*)**: powerful planetary combinations or positions representing authority, power, and success
- **Rashi (*rah-shee*)**: another term for the zodiac signs; there are 12 of them, each occupying 0 degrees of the entire zodiac.
- **Remedies**: rituals or practices performed to reduce or eliminate a planet's negative influences. This can include mantras, gemstones, prayers, charitable acts, and so on.
- **Rising Sign**: see Lagna

S
- **Sandhi*: (suhn-dhee):*** this Sanskrit term describes the concept of merging or joining. In Vedic astrology, it is used to reference the junction or transitional phase between two houses or signs. It is a sensitive zone that can influence the effects and interpretation of the planetary positions and the energy flow between different life aspects.
- **Sanskrit (*suhn-skrit*)**: sacred language in Jainism, Buddhism, and Hinduism, used in multiple scriptures and texts.
- **Sanyasi (*suhn-yuh-see*)**: someone who has declared themselves free of material possessions and gone down the spiritual path instead.
- **Saptamamsha (*suhp-tuh-muhm-shuh*)**: the D-7 chart is another divisional/Varga chart that helps provide information about an individual's children. It is used when evaluating their 5th house in the birth chart.
- **Saptvishansh (*suhp-tuh-vee-shahn-shuh*)**: refers to a divisional chart called D-27, used in the analysis of an individual's

capabilities and strength based on the positions of the planets.

- **Shadvarga (*shuhd-vuhr-guh*)**: translates to six charts, which are the Hora, Drekkana, Saptamsha, Navamsha, Dwadamsha, and Vishamsha. The most important of these is the Navamsha, which is typically used with the Rashi chart.
- **Shashtyamsa (*shuhsh-tee-uhm-suh*)**: otherwise known as the D-60, this Varga/divisional chart determines good or bad events in a person's life.
- **Shirshodaya (*sheer-shoh-dah-yuh*)**: signs that rise in the East during sunrise; the signs are Aquarius, Gemini, Leo, Libra, Scorpio, and Virgo.
- **Shodasamsa (*shoh-duh-suhm-suh*)**: the D-16 chart is a divisional/Varga chart that helps an astrologer get more information on luxuries, accidents, trouble, and vehicle-related death in an individual's birth chart.
- **Shukla Paksha (*shook-luh puhk-shuh*)**: the light half of the lunar month, when the Moon waxes.
- **Sidereal Zodiac (*sy-deer-ee-uhl zoh-dee-ak*)**: the fixed zodiac is used the most in Vedic astrology, as it indicates the real constellations and their movements at a given time.
- **Sign:** a zodiac constellation.
- **Sthira (*sthee-ruh*)**: the fixed signs.

T

- **Tajika (*tuh-jee-kuh*)**: these are the Vedic equivalent of the major aspects used in Western astrology – Conjunction, Opposition, Square, Trine, and Sextile. They measure the aspects between the planets rather than between planets and signs.
- **Trik (*trihk*)**: collectively the 6th, 8th and 12th, or inauspicious houses – see Dusthana.
- **Trimasamsa (*tree-muh-suhm-suh*)**: this is a different kind of divisional chart. It is the 30th Harmonic, but it doesn't seem to have much to do with dividing a sign by 30. There are five divisions, none of them equal, and there is no mention of Leo or Cancer. However, it does give important information about health issues and bad luck.

- **Trishansh** (*trih-shahn-shuh*): the D-30 is a divisional/Varga chart used by an astrologer to determine the challenges a problem an individual may be facing in the future. This can indicate bad health, bad luck, and problems ahead.
- **Tropical Zodiac:** this is the zodiac typically used by Western astrologers and is known as the "moving" zodiac; unlike Sidereal astrology, it doesn't use natural constellations.

U

- **Ubhayodaya** (*oob-huh-yoh-dah-yuh*): a both-rising planet with some characteristics of a front-rising planet and some of a back-riser. There is only one planet – Pisces.
- **Upachaya** (*oo-puh-chuh-yuh*): collectively the 3rd, 6th, 10th, and 11th houses. Upachaya translates to "improving" because the planets in those houses increase their influence and strength over time. This is especially the case with the 11th house.
- **Upagrahas** (*oo-puh-gruh-huhs*): these are additional mathematical points or planetary bodies used in Vedic astrology, representing certain conditions or influences, i.e., Mandi (financial) and Gulka (misfortune).

V

- **Varga Charts:** these are divisional charts used by Vedic astrologers to provide more insight into certain aspects of an individual's life. Each chart focuses on a certain aspect.
- **Vata** (*vuh-tuh*): this dosha in Ayurveda is ruled by a combination of air and space (ether).
- **Vedic Astrology:** see Jyotish.
- **Vimshotari Dasha** (*vim-shoh-tuh-ree duh-shuh*): the most commonly used Dasha system, also called the Udu Dasha.
- **Vishamsa** (*vee-shahm-suh*): the D-20 chart is a divisional/Varga chart used by an astrologer to determine details about an indovodiaul's spiritual and religious inclinations.

Y

- **Yoga** (*yoh-guh*): in Jyotish, yoga indicates a combination, typically of at least two planets or a planet/sign, or planet/house, usually involving another planet's aspect. More than two planets will sometimes be involved.

- **Yogakaraka** (*yoh-guh-kah-ruh-kuh*): this is a significantly strong planet that creates auspicious combinations of yogas in an individual's birth chart. This planet can bring success, prosperity, and positive outcomes.

Z

- **Zodiac:** this consists of twelve divisions equally spaced in a 360-degree circle. Each 30-degree division is named for a certain constellation, and these are known as Rashis in Vedic astrology.

Conclusion

Thanks for reading" The Lunar Nodes: Unlock the Secrets of the Navagrahas, Your Birth Chart, Karma, the Sun and Moon in Astrology, and the Twelve Houses of the Zodiac." It is hoped that you enjoyed it and have learned something new.

Vedic astrology is completely different from Western astrology, and exploring the lunar nodes gives you the perfect opportunity to understand the Navagrahas and unlock their secrets. You also get a deeper understanding of the twelve houses and their role in the zodiac and your life.

Rahu and Ketu, the lunar nodes, are significant in Vedic astrology, representing ambition and desire (Rahu) and liberation and detachment (Ketu.) Understanding the lunar nodes in relation to your birth chart can help you understand what lessons you should learn from this lifetime and the karmic imprints from your past lives. You should now understand that the twelve houses represent different aspects of your life. While each focuses on a specific area, looking at all twelve can give you the perfect overview of your life.

All of this allows you to understand your life, discover hidden patterns, understand your karmic journey, and make the right choices in life. You can now live more consciously, understand your real potential and take the right path with better self-awareness and wisdom.

You have undertaken an incredibly spiritual journey in this book, but this is only the beginning. Take some time to improve your understanding and learn how the lunar nodes influence your life.

Here's another book by Mari Silva that you might like

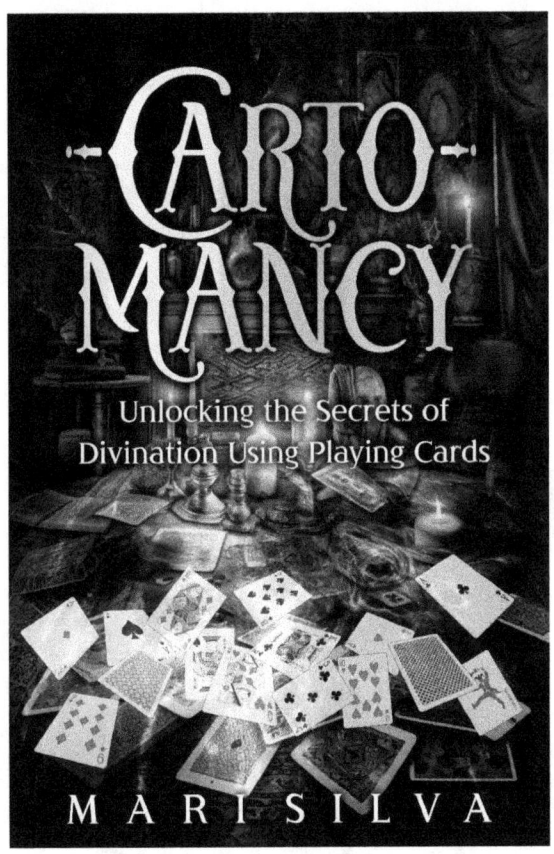

Your Free Gift
(only available for a limited time)

Thanks for getting this book! If you want to learn more about various spirituality topics, then join Mari Silva's community and get a free guided meditation MP3 for awakening your third eye. This guided meditation mp3 is designed to open and strengthen ones third eye so you can experience a higher state of consciousness. Simply visit the link below the image to get started.

https://spiritualityspot.com/meditation

Or, Scan the QR code!

References

""As You Sow so Shall You Reap" Karma Astrology Works in That Way Darling!" GaneshaSpeaks, www.ganeshaspeaks.com/predictions/astrology/fruits-of-karma/.

"CHARACTERISTICS of the TWELVE HOUSES in ASTROLOGY." Vedic Astro Zone, 1 Apr. 2017, vedicastrozone.com/characteristics-of-the-twelve-houses-in-astrology/. .

"Decoding the Different Types of Birth Chart Formats." Jothishi, 2 Oct. 2020, jothishi.com/different-birth-chart-formats/.

"Don't Resonate with Your Sun Sign? Give Vedic Astrology a Try." Cosmopolitan, 6 Apr. 2022, www.cosmopolitan.com/lifestyle/a39642096/vedic-astrology/.

"Eclipsing Effects of Rahu and Ketu in Astrology." GaneshaSpeaks, www.ganeshaspeaks.com/astrology/planets/nodes/.

"Essentials of Vedic Astrology: Elements & Basic Principles." Jothishi, 20 Sept. 2019, jothishi.com/essentials-of-vedic-astrology/#:~:text=came%20into%20being.-

"Everything You Need to Know about Sidereal Astrology." Thought Catalog, Thought Catalog, 15 Jan. 2019, thoughtcatalog.com/january-nelson/2019/01/sidereal-astrology/.

"Houses in Horoscope- Bhava, Houses in Your Birth Chart, 12 Astrology Houses." Www.astrodevam.com, www.astrodevam.com/knowledge-bank/bhavas-houses.html.

"How to Interpret North Nodes & South Nodes to Find Your True Purpose." Mindbodygreen, 28 Dec. 2020, www.mindbodygreen.com/articles/astrology-101-north-nodes-south-nodes-reveal-your-life-purpose#:~:text=Astrologers%20use%20the%20lunar%20nodes.

"Moon's Nodes." Www.astro.com, www.astro.com/astrology/in_dg_node_e.htm.

"Navagraha - the Nine Planets in Hindu Astrology - Effects, Elements, Temple Details." TemplePurohit - Your Spiritual Destination | Bhakti, Shraddha Aur Ashirwad, 15 Mar. 2019, www.templepurohit.com/navagraha-nine-planets-hinduism-astrology/.

"Navagrahas." Myths and Folklore Wiki, mythus.fandom.com/wiki/Navagrahas.

"Outlook India Magazine Online- Read Today's News India, Latest News Analysis, World, Sports, Entertainment | Best Online Magazine India." www.outlookindia.com/.

"Remedies - Effective Astrological Remedies to Improve Life!" Www.astroyogi.com, www.astroyogi.com/remedies#:~:text=What%20is%20the%20Astrological%20Remedy.

"Rising Sign Calculator - Find Your Ascendant Sign." GaneshaSpeaks, www.ganeshaspeaks.com/kundli-ascendant-sign.

"Significance of Navagraha." GaneshaSpeaks, www.ganeshaspeaks.com/predictions/astrology/navagraha/.

"Understanding the Houses in Vedic Astrology." Vinay Bajrangi, www.vinaybajrangi.com/astrology-houses.php.

"What Are Karmic Debt Numbers? All about Karmic Debt Numbers." Astrotalk, astrotalk.com/numerology-introduction/karmic-debt.

"What Is Karmic Astrology? | Zodiac Psychics Blog." Www.zodiacpsychics.com, www.zodiacpsychics.com/article/what-is-karmic-astrology.html.

Astrology, Om. "Yogas and Doshas in Birth Chart/Horoscope - Indian Vedic Astrology." Om Astrology, www.omastrology.com/indian-vedic-astrology/yogas-doshas/.

Door, Ayurveda Next. "How to Read Your Vedic Birth Chart in 5 Easy...." Spirituality+Health, 9 Nov. 2015, www.spiritualityhealth.com/articles/2015/11/09/how-read-your-vedic-birth-chart-5-easy-steps.

"What Is Vedic Astrology? Learn the Signs, Planets, Nakshatras & More." Popular Vedic Science, 10 Oct. 2019, popularvedicscience.com/astrology/what-is-astrology/.

Kelly, Aliza. "Astrology Birth Charts 101." The Cut, 22 Aug. 2022, www.thecut.com/article/astrology-birth-chart-meaning-analysis.html#:~:text=An%20astrological%20birth%20chart%20%E2%80%94%20also.

Mukherjee, Sayani. "A Brief Introduction to Nakshatra Analysis." Vedic Astrology, 15 Nov. 2018, artofdivinescience.wordpress.com/2018/11/15/a-brief-introduction-to-nakshatra-analysis/.

Sirdesai, Narayan. "Karma and Economics." The Economic Times, 14 Oct. 2022, economictimes.indiatimes.com/opinion/speaking-tree/karma-and-economics/articleshow/94845689.cms?from=mdr.

Stardust, Lisa. "Literally Everything You Need to Know about Understanding Nodes in Your Birth Chart." Cosmopolitan, 26 Jan. 2022, www.cosmopolitan.com/lifestyle/a30198931/north-south-node-meaning-placement-birth-chart/.

Thomas, Kyle. "What Exactly Is an "Aspect" in Astrology?" Cosmopolitan, 15 Mar. 2022, www.cosmopolitan.com/lifestyle/a37341996/astrology-aspects-list/.